The Land and Government of Muscovy

A SIXTEENTH-CENTURY ACCOUNT

Tsar Ivan IV

Heinrich von Staden

The Land and Government of Muscovy

A SIXTEENTH-CENTURY ACCOUNT

Translated and Edited
by THOMAS ESPER

Stanford University Press · Stanford, California · 1967

This book is a translation of four sixteenth-century German manu-
scripts, which were first published in Russian by Andrei Polosin (Moscow, 1925). The present edition was translated from Fritz Epstein,
ed., Heinrich von Staden, *Aufzeichnungen über den Moskauer Staat*
(Hamburg, 1930).

Stanford University Press
Stanford, California
© *1967 by the Board of Trustees of the*
Leland Stanford Junior University
Printed in the United States of America
L.C. 67-17301

Translator's Note

The original text of the Staden documents is semiliterate and incredibly disjointed. Actually, the only copy we have (which is presently in the State Archives of Lower Saxony in Hannover) was copied from the original manuscript by someone other than the author, and a number of errors and omissions were the result of rapid and careless copying. However, Staden himself is most to blame. The style is often the affectation of a scarcely learned person who wishes to seem elegant; hence the stilted passages, especially the addresses to Rudolf, the Holy Roman Emperor. At other times a crude colloquialism alternates with abrupt statements of fact. Little effort was made at transition between paragraphs or even sentences. I have done what I could to make the text smoother without distorting the author's meaning. And to this purpose I have inserted additional words and passages in brackets to assist the reader. Longer explanations are placed in footnotes. Important persons and words are identified at first occurrence, which can be easily located in the Index. I have used the modified Library of Congress system for transliterating personal names and other Russian words. The British system is used for all place names. All miles in the text are German miles, and are not accurate (each "mile" may be three to seven English miles or more).

The reader who wishes a definitive edition of Staden's text is reminded of Fritz Epstein's exhaustive work (see footnote 2 to the Introduction). The text of that edition is in the original sixteenth-century German, and may be too difficult for persons with a modest command of the language. The notes to the text, however, are clear and extremely useful.

I should like to express my special gratitude to Professor Michael Cherniavsky, who encouraged me in this task.

T.E.

Contents

Introduction

Heinrich von Staden's account of the state of affairs in Muscovy was written in late 1578 and 1579, not long after the author returned from there to Western Europe. (He may have returned during the summer of 1576.) It is not a traveler's account, like Baron von Herberstein's,[1] nor is it a history; and it was not intended for publication. The four parts of the Staden documents—the petition, the description of Muscovy, the proposal for an invasion of Muscovy, and the autobiography—were submitted to Rudolf II, the Holy Roman Emperor, with the advice that they be kept secret. We do not know whether Rudolf ever saw them.

From Staden's point of view the most important part of the account was his proposal for an invasion of Muscovy. The other parts were merely supporting material: the petition is an introduction, the description of Muscovy demonstrates Staden's knowledge of Russian affairs, the autobiography introduces Staden and recounts his experience. Staden hoped to persuade the Emperor to

[1] R. H. Major, ed., Sigismund von Herberstein, *Notes Upon Russia* (London: Hakluyt Society, volumes 10 and 12, 1851 and 1852). Herberstein's is the major foreign account of Russia in the sixteenth century. It describes the reign of Vasilii III (1505–33). It was published in 1549 and went through many editions in several languages.

undertake the conquest of Muscovite Russia, and despite his claim to the contrary, he evidently anticipated some reward for his part in such a project.

Anyone who has the most modest understanding of the military and diplomatic affairs of late-sixteenth-century Europe will see that Staden's invasion proposal is a harebrained scheme. And the supporting documents will indicate why Staden could never have gained high princely preferment—he was a brutish adventurer, unsophisticated in matters of state. Still, the proposed invasion was taken seriously by some, and Staden was employed for a while by a prince who hoped to carry out a similar project.

Georg Hans von Veldenz-Lützelstein, Count of the Palatinate, although the prince of a rather insignificant realm, was related to the Swedish royal house. He was an ambitious man who strove to increase his importance by formulating sweeping plans for building an Imperial fleet and conquering Muscovite Russia. Tsar Ivan IV (the Terrible) of Russia had invaded the eastern Baltic region called Livonia in 1558, and this contributed to the disintegration of the Livonian Order of Knights, who ruled that area, a few years later. In 1578 the war still raged, with the Russians controlling a major portion of the country. Although Livonia was legally part of the Holy Roman Empire and deserved Imperial defense, the Empire as a whole was more concerned with the Turkish danger. Within the Empire, the Russians were considered more a potential ally against the Turks than an invader of Imperial territory. Thus, the Empire took no serious action in the Livonian war—beyond resolutions of support to the Livonians, small contributions, and attempts at mediation. Princes of northern Germany, however, as well as the Swedes and Poles who were fighting the Russians in Livonia, were more concerned with the Muscovite threat than with the Turkish threat. Count Georg Hans, although a south German prince, was a member of the anti-Russian faction because of his ambitions and his marital ties to the Swedish royal house.

Staden's account reflects the fear and the division of opinion regarding Russia that existed in Germany. He at times declares that Ivan wished to conquer the Holy Roman Empire; but most often he emphasizes Russia's weakness. If the Tatars conquered Russia, Staden reasoned, the Turkish danger would be extended to northern Europe, because the Crimean Khan was a vassal of the Turkish Sultan. There is consequently a contradiction in Staden's assessment of Russia's strength: it is both a threat to the Empire and too weak to withstand the Tatars. Staden thus appeals to both interest groups.

Between 1578 and 1582, Count Georg Hans sought to build an anti-Russian coalition composed of the German Order of Knights, Sweden, and Poland. (The German Order was the successor of the Livonian Order, but its land holdings were insignificant and were all in western Germany.) These European forces would together attack Ivan IV from the north by sea, while the Tatars would invade from across the steppe land in the south. The purpose of this concerted effort was to force the Russians out of Livonia and to restore that region to the German Order. Heinrich von Staden was very much involved in those plans. In 1578 he was sent to the Master of the German Order (and later to the Polish and the Swedish courts) on behalf of Count Georg Hans. He evidently carried with him a proposal for an invasion of northern Russia by sea. Nothing ever came of this scheme, and historians were unaware of it until 1893, when the proposal was discovered in the Prussian state archives. Staden's participation in the coalition effort was unknown (the Staden documents were still to be discovered), and the entire project was ascribed to Count Georg Hans. When the Staden documents turned up a few years later in the state archives in Hannover, it became apparent that the Count's project was a variation of Staden's. A third version was recently found; it had been presented to King John III of Sweden, probably in 1581 but possibly in 1591. All three versions are contained in the second edition of Fritz Epstein's masterly work on the Staden documents, to which, of course, I am greatly in debt.[2]

The most elaborate of the three versions of the Muscovy invasion plan is the one published here, although the one sent to the Master of the German Order may have been written earlier; the one submitted to the King of Sweden was certainly a later version. Little is known about the circumstances in which Staden presented the last version to the Swedes, but it seems that he was acting on his own behalf, because he requested a place in Swedish service. The plan translated here was obviously proposed independently of Count Georg Hans, because Staden indicates that he had only been in that prince's service for several months, and suggests that he was no longer employed. Thus, it seems that Staden and Count Georg Hans first conceived the project together, and then Staden attempted to sell it independently.

[2] Fritz Epstein, ed., Heinrich von Staden, *Aufzeichnungen über den Moskauer Staat* (Hamburg: Friederichsen, De Gruyter & Co. m.b.H., 1930). Second edition (Hamburg: Cram, De Gruyter & Co., 1964).

Although the Staden documents were primarily written as an invasion plan, the plan itself is of less historical value to us than the supporting materials, particularly the description of Muscovy and Staden's autobiography. From these portions of the documents we gain a fresh insight into the very troubled, dramatic, and confusing affairs of Muscovy in the late 1560's and early 1570's. There are few firsthand accounts of this period, and of those that do exist Staden's is by far the best.[3] The reason for this superiority is Staden's desire to write a description of Muscovy rather than a propagandistic tract denouncing that state and its prince. Perhaps one reason Staden refrained from a full-scale denunciation of Ivan's brutality—the dominant theme in other accounts of this period—is that Staden was himself an extremely brutish person. He describes, for example, how he cut down a harmless woman with an axe as an interesting, if not valorous, episode. He recounts other instances of his cruelty similarly, without excuses or embarrassment. Staden calls Ivan a horrid tyrant, but he probably admired him. This quality of Staden's character permitted him to write more

---

[3] Other well-known accounts are those of Prince Kurbskii and of Johann Taube and Elert Kruse: J. L. I. Fennell, ed., *The Correspondence between Prince A. M. Kurbsky and Tsar Ivan IV of Russia 1564–1579* (Cambridge: Cambridge University Press, 1963); J. L. I. Fennell, ed., *Kurbsky's History of Ivan IV* (Cambridge: Cambridge University Press, 1965). Johann Taube and Elert Kruse, "Sendschreiben an Gotthard Kettler, Herzog zu Kurland und Semgallen, 1572," *Sammlung russischer Geschichte*, X, Part 1 (Dorpat, 1816), pp. 185–238. Kurbskii defected to Sigismund August of Poland-Lithuania in 1564; Taube and Kruse deserted in 1571. Both the former and the latter wrote about Russia in such a way as to justify their behavior: they depicted Tsar Ivan and his government as unworthy of the loyal services of honorable men. Their accounts are much more clearly biased than Staden's.

dispassionately about Russian affairs than any of his contemporaries; and for that reason his account is more balanced.

Staden's description of the Muscovite administration is valuable as an interesting firsthand account, and because it helps corroborate other sources; but it contains no new facts. Still, his account of the oprichnina, a peculiar state within the state created by Ivan IV in 1565, is the only one in existence written by one of its members (Staden was mistaken in considering Johann Taube and Elert Kruse members of the oprichnina; they were actually diplomatic agents). The major advantage of this account as an historical source is Staden's lack of emphasis on Ivan's terroristic behavior against Russian nobles. Other accounts concentrated on this to such an extent that historians for a long while believed that the oprichnina was an attempt to destroy the Russian aristocracy to the advantage of the petty service nobility. From Staden's account it is clear that the terror was used more selectively, that aristocrats in their traditional order of rank were members of the oprichnina, and that Ivan was settling scores with specific individuals and factions that he considered dangerous to his exalted conception of autocracy, and not with an entire class. The history of the oprichnina has been rewritten since the publication of Staden's account.

No pre-Revolutionary Russian historians used the Staden documents, because they were discovered only in this century and were not published until I. I. Polosin brought out his Russian translation in 1925.[4] In 1930 a definitive

---

[4] Heinrich von Staden, *O Moskve Ivana Groznogo*, translated and edited by I. I. Polosin (Moscow: M. & S. Sabashnikovykh, 1925). Polosin's edition is a rather good translation but its annotation does not approach Epstein's.

edition with the original German text exhaustively an-
notated was published by Fritz Epstein. A second edition
of this work, somewhat expanded but not actually re-
vised, was published in 1964. Since the publication of the
Staden documents, all serious historians writing of the
reign of Ivan the Terrible have used them.

The oprichnina was not an entirely fortuitous develop-
ment.[5] Its roots extended back into the history of Russia,
to Ivan III (1462–1505), who expanded the principality
of Moscow into an extensive Russian empire. The "gath-
ering of the Russian lands" around Moscow involved
the subjugation of numerous princely houses to the authority of the grand prince of Moscow. This process of
political consolidation continued during the reign of Vasilii III (1505–33), and when the infant Ivan IV suc-
ceeded his father in 1533, the only areas with a Russian
population but outside Muscovite control were those subject to the Polish-Lithuanian monarch.

The previously independent princely houses of Russia were not exterminated, but were merely deprived of
their sovereign authority; their members became servitor
princes of the Muscovite grand princes, who beginning in
1547 assumed the title of tsar. The servitor princes and
the old Muscovite boyars exercised the highest civil and
military authority in this new state. Their rank in service
was regulated by an extremely complex system of se-

[5] The oprichnina has been a challenge to historical interpretation
for generations. For a thorough historiographical study of this subject
see A. A. Zimin, *Oprichnina Ivana Groznogo* (Moscow, 1964),
pp. 7–80. Zimin's work is the best history of this period of Ivan the
Terrible's reign. It is a continuation of an earlier study, *Reformy
Ivana Groznogo* (Moscow, 1960). For a discussion of the ideological
basis of the oprichnina see Bjarne Nørretranders, *The Shaping of
Czardom under Ivan Groznyi* (Copenhagen, 1964).

niority, *mestnichestvo*, which was a constant cause of squabbling among the ruling aristocrats. Although the princes had lost their former sovereign status, as a corporate group under the tsar they continued to rule the larger unified Russian state. They recognized the autocratic authority of Ivan III and Vasilii III, but there remained considerable ambiguity about the true extent of that authority. The aristocrats, for example, insisted on their right to serve in strict conformity to the principle of mestnichestvo, by which the grand prince had no authority to appoint a person to a commanding position unless all those serving under him were lower on the scale of seniority. Thus the grand prince was unable to appoint the most suitable or talented persons to serve as his civil and military commanders. Furthermore, a number of the aristocrats maintained considerable military forces of their own. From the death of Vasilii III in 1533 to the coronation of Ivan IV as tsar in 1547—that is, during Ivan's minority—the faction-ridden aristocrats ruled Russia, and their internal struggles resulted in considerable disorder. During this period little deference was shown the young grand prince, and his wealth was plundered by greedy nobles. Ivan never forgot these indignities.

The young monarch, when crowned tsar, did not assume his office as an upholder of the status quo. His realm was in need of reform and his position within the structure of Russian society was, to him, inadequate. Ivan's early years were occupied with the subjugation of the khanate of Kazan, located on the middle Volga; it finally fell in 1552. The khanate of Astrakhan, in the delta of the Volga, was conquered a few years later. With the entire course of the Volga under Muscovite control, the

xvi

eastern frontier was both secure and open to further expansion. In addition to military victories, the first decade of Ivan's rule brought financial and administrative reforms, a new law code, and military reform. This progressive government was not actually Ivan's creation; his close advisors were responsible for it. In general, reform measures were possible only because of a moderation exercised both by the aristocrats and by the sovereign. This policy of compromise was seriously disturbed in 1553, when it appeared that Ivan was dying, and the aristocrats expressed reluctance to swear allegiance to his infant son, preferring Ivan's cousin Vladimir Andreevich. Ivan, who soon recovered, did not wreak vengeance on his disobedient servitors, and the progressive policies of the government were continued; but in later years he referred to this episode as one of many indications of aristocratic perfidy, although the nobles had good reason for wanting to avoid another long regency.

The autocrat and the aristocrats were successful in their policy of compromise only so long as the reformist measures that were adopted did not seriously violate the interests of either side. Therefore, in 1558, when Ivan began the Livonian war, which promised long hardship and great expense (for it meant war with Lithuania), the aristocrats became disaffected. They would have preferred military action against the source of more immediate danger in the south, the khanate of the Crimea. The war so increased the power of the monarch that the former balance of interests was upset; and soon after the war began, Ivan became estranged from those advisors who were most responsible for the policy of compromise. It was in this condition of growing autocratic power that a number of distinguished aristocrats deserted, many going to the enemy state, Poland-Lithuania. The most serious defection came in 1564 from Prince Andrei Kurbskii, the commander of the Russian forces in Livonia and long a trusted friend of the Tsar. It is not surprising that Ivan became extremely suspicious of all the aristocrats, and recalled in his letters to Kurbskii, who was now in the enemy camp, all the past indignities and treacherous behavior he had suffered at their hands.

Without warning, in December 1564 (a few months after Kurbskii deserted), Ivan left Moscow with an unusually large retinue. He eventually arrived at Aleksandrova Sloboda, and dispatched a message announcing his abdication. He gave as his reason the disloyalty and dishonesty of the princes and boyars, and in another message declared to the common people of Moscow that he had no complaints or charges against them. The people of Moscow, who viewed the Tsar as their protector against aristocratic arbitrariness, sent a delegation to plead for his return. Ivan relented only on the condition that he be permitted to establish a private realm within the state, where he could live surrounded by especially loyal servitors, that he be given a free hand to deal with the traitorous and corrupt aristocrats, and that he receive from his subjects an indemnity of 100,000 rubles, a monstrous sum. These conditions were agreed to, and Ivan set up the oprichnina.

The oprichnina was designed to provide the Tsar with protection and to serve as a base from which the most dangerous of the aristocrats could be destroyed. It encompassed a considerable amount of territory, not all of it contiguous, and it grew as the years passed. Heinrich von Staden's description of this special royal domain is essentially correct, although he did not fully understand the reason for its creation: the ideological struggle over the nature of the Russian autocracy.

The oprichnina was conceived as a solution to the conflict between Ivan's views of his role in society and the aristocrats' views of theirs. Ivan believed that he was answerable to no one but God, and that the aristocrats were no less his subjects than the most humble peasants. The aristocrats, while recognizing the Tsar's supreme authority, insisted upon their special privileges and rights as a corporate group, believing that they, in some ill-defined manner, shared with Ivan the rule of Muscovy. When Ivan began to act in an overbearing manner, they accused him of arbitrariness. And when the aristocrats, supported by the higher clergy, opposed the Tsar's autocratic behavior, Ivan reacted harshly, leading some princes and boyars into treason.

The oprichnina continued as a recognizable institution until 1572. During the seven years of its existence, the most independent and powerful aristocrats were either killed, financially ruined, or cowed; the last vestiges of separatist sentiment in Novgorod were destroyed; and the independence of the Church was attacked, though not much diminished. Thus, Ivan's policy was in one respect successful: his authority emerged unchallenged. But it can also be argued that the price paid for victory was inordinately high. The special forces of the oprichnina, as Staden clearly shows, slipped from Ivan's control and ravaged the *zemshchina*—that part of Muscovy outside the oprichnina. This left the country a shambles, and accounted to a great extent for the burning of Moscow by the Crimean Tatars in 1571, and ultimately, for the loss of the Livonian war. Ivan was compelled to turn against his leading servitors in the oprichnina, who were guilty not only of plundering but perhaps even of treason; they were executed and the oprichnina was abolished. Years later, after Ivan's death, the English observer Giles Fletcher noted that the enmities aroused during the oprichnina period still smoldered, and would be likely to lead Russia into civil war. Civil war did in fact occur at the beginning of the seventeenth century.

Heinrich von Staden was the son of a burgomaster from the small town of Ahlen in Westphalia. He was born within a year or two of 1545, but we have no idea when he died. From his autobiography it appears that Staden was a troublemaker in his youth and an unprincipled adventurer in his adult years. Because of his bad behavior at home in Ahlen, around 1560 he was shipped out of town to relatives in the German city of Riga on the eastern Baltic. At that time Riga and the entire territory of Livonia were involved in a war with Tsar Ivan IV.

Staden briefly describes his five-year stay in Livonia, probably with considerable exaggeration, and then tells of his passage into Russian service and his career as a member of Ivan the Terrible's oprichnina. Staden's career in Russia, as it is described in his account, raises some questions. He claimed that he was granted estates immediately upon entering Ivan's service. But what could a nineteen- or twenty-year-old have offered the Tsar of all Russia? Despite this incongruity, we must assume that he was indeed taken into service and given estates. Yet he boasted further, "There were only four of us Germans in the court of the Grand Prince's oprichnina." He thus even intimated that he was accepted into the oprichnina as soon as he settled in Moscow. Epstein apparently accepted Staden's claims, because he not only failed to question them, but indeed dismissed Polosin's attempt to explain that Staden first came to Russia as some sort of official merchant and recruiter of foreign specialists.[6] Polosin was probably correct in maintaining that Staden was an interpreter for a while. According to his own account, Staden knew German, Latin, Latvian, and Russian. Polosin did not accept Staden's intimation that he was an oprichnik from the time of his arrival or close to it, but he was uncertain about when Staden was taken into the oprichnina. An examination of Staden's text seems to indicate that he was employed in lesser tasks in the zemshchina until he became an oprichnik—which was shortly before the arrival of Duke Magnus (in the first half of 1570) and at the time Staritsa was taken into the oprichnina (not later than 1569)—that is to say, in late 1569.

Although Polosin makes some guesses, what Staden did before joining the oprichnina is uncertain. He indicated that he owned taverns and that he had important friends both before and after becoming an oprichnik. Since A. Muliukin has demonstrated that foreigners were only permitted to reside in Muscovy if they were merchants, clerics, or government employees, one thing is certain: Staden must have been employed by Ivan in some manner.[7] Staden described his private ventures eagerly, but he only indirectly mentioned his official duties. Perhaps he was not satisfied with that aspect of his career. What we can learn from his autobiography indicates that this was most probably the case: "I was then constantly

---

[6] In the introduction to *Aufzeichnungen über den Moskauer Staat*, p. 24*n.

[7] A. Muliukin, "O svobode priezda inostrantsev v Moskovskoe gosudarstvo," *Zhurnal Ministerstva Narodnago Prosveshcheniia*, XV, new series (1908), 57–81.

with the chief boyar, Ivan Petrovich Cheliadnin, and was helping a Pole translate a German herbal book into Russian." And again: "I stood not far from Wilhelm Fürstenberg and the interpreter, Caspar von Wittenberg, in order to hear if the interpreter translated correctly." In both of these cases Staden's position was insignificant—he was simply assisting others in minor tasks. The major portion of his autobiography, nevertheless, is concerned with his career in the oprichnina; and that career was quite short, lasting for less than three years, not six years as Polosin suggested.[8] The question remains: how did Staden become an oprichnik?

In December of 1569 Ivan began his expedition against Novgorod and Pskov. When he returned, he executed some of his closest collaborators in the oprichnina—including Aleksei and Fedor Basmanov, Nikita Funikov, and Ivan Viskovatyi—130 persons in all. Those people were implicated in a conspiracy with Novgorod, and their executions were part of Ivan's measures against that city. Perhaps Staden was taken into the oprichnina in anticipation of this confrontation with the conspirators. The young German was known around Moscow, it appears from his account, even before he became an oprichnik. If Ivan was indeed strengthening his position in expectation of a serious conspiracy, it would not have been unusual for him to take Staden and other unattached people into the oprichnina, as members of his personal corps. Once the danger of the conspiracy was past, the Tatar threat overcome, and the country reunified following Ivan's reconciliation with the zemshchina, Staden's services would not have been needed. Thus, Staden was taken on in desperate times, and was never an important

---

[8] In *O Moskve Ivana Groznogo*, p. 51.

person in the oprichnina. The fact that he was "forgotten in the mustering" in 1572 can be explained by his insignificance.

From his own account it appears that Staden knew little about military affairs. He presented himself as a soldier in Russian service, and as a person of such experience that he could seriously present a plan for the invasion of Muscovy. But his failure to mention such essential information as the size of the Russian forces and the sort of equipment and armament they used, and his failure to devote more than a few lines to military organization, can only suggest a lack of knowledge of these matters. Only two episodes in his account can be considered to be of a military sort. If he served in the army at all (and he probably did at least briefly), it was in a modest capacity.

If Staden was never a very important person in the oprichnina, another question arises. How did he, scarcely more than a youth, manage to prosper as he evidently did? His account suggests that it was through the patronage of powerful persons, such as Ivan IV and Fedor Basmanov. However, it is necessary to understand that Staden exaggerated his role in the oprichnina in order to pose as an important authority on Russian affairs, and he was probably not the close friend of the great that he claimed to be.

Regardless of the fact that Staden's account is highly tendentious, and despite occasional factual errors in it (which resulted largely from contradictions between Staden's actual insignificant position and the importance he strove to give himself), it is a highly valuable source for the study of Russia during the years of the oprichnina.

The Land and Government of Muscovy
A SIXTEENTH-CENTURY ACCOUNT

Western Border of Muscovite Russia, about 1584

BARENTS SEA

Pechenga monastery
Kola
LAPLAND
Pustozersk
Pechora R.

Kandalaksha
TERSKIY NOS
SAMOYEDS

SWEDEN
KARELIA
WHITE SEA
Lampozhnya

Solovetskii monastery
Arkhangelsk
Kholmogory

FINLAND
Onega R.
N. Duina R.

BALTIC SEA

Lake Ladoga
Lake Onega
Solvychegodsk

FINNISH GULF
Vyborg
Kargopol

Reval
Beloye Ozero
Kirillo monastery
Dorpat
Belozersk
Vologda

Gauya R.
Novgorod
Lake Ilmen

Riga
Wenden
Pskov
Rybnaya Sloboda

W. Duina R.
LIVONIA
Torzhok
Volga R.

Vilna
Toropets
Tver
Yaroslavl

Troitskii monastery †
Pereyaslavl-zaleski
Gorodets
Volga R.

Vitebsk
Vyazma
Moscow
Aleksandrova Sloboda
Nizhny Novgorod
Kazan

Smolensk
Sviyazhsk

Oka R.

Belev
Tula
RYAZAN LAND

Kiev

Don R.

Dnieper R.

Volga R.

Donets R.

CRIMEAN KHANATE
Azov
NOGAI TATARS
Astrakhan

BLACK SEA
Bakhchisaray
CIRCASSIAN LAND
CASPIAN SEA

I. *Petition* [*to the Emperor Rudolf*]

To your Majesty, Roman Emperor, King of Hungary and Bohemia, our most gracious lord, most humbly and obediently, I, Heinrich von Staden, present this petition.

Most illustrious, all-powerful, unconquerable Roman Emperor, King of Hungary and Bohemia, our most gracious lord!

How Russia has hitherto been ruled; how the princes held their own lands, the *votchiny* and *pomestia*;[1] how they war against their country's hereditary foe, the Crimean Khan;[2] where they usually encounter him; how extensively the Crimean Khan has devastated the country; how he burned Moscow; and how vigorously he strives to conquer Russia and to carry off the Grand

---

[1] *Votchiny* (sing. *votchina*) were patrimonial estates traditionally not held on service tenure. Beginning in the middle 1550's, however, holders of votchiny were required to render military service to the tsar. *Pomestia* (sing. *pomest'e*) were government lands awarded in exchange for service. In the course of the seventeenth century, pomestia became inheritable, at least de facto.

[2] The Crimean Khan at that time was Devlet-Girei, 1551–78. The empire of the Golden Horde began to collapse with the death of Tamerlane in 1405. By the turn of the sixteenth century, the Tatars of the Crimea had become the most serious threat to Muscovy's southern frontiers. They raided and pillaged deep in the Muscovite realm, hoping to reestablish Tatar suzerainty over Russia.

I

Prince[3] and his two sons into the Crimea and deprive him of his treasure—these things your Imperial Roman Majesty will find in this my written description. I have also written in this report that the Grand Prince has had the rulers of his own land murdered without pity and mercy, how this happened, and how the omnipotent God punished the country with famine and pestilence, as well as how other things came to pass.

I give this account in order that the Crimean Khan's plans [to conquer Russia] shall fail. He is supported by the Turkish Sultan, the people of Kazan and Astrakhan, the Nogais, the Tatars, and Prince Mikhail Cherkasskii; I do not include the King of Poland since he is just as dependent upon the Turkish Sultan as the Crimean Khan is.[4] Because the merciful God has so often and won-

---

[3] The Grand Prince was Tsar Ivan IV, who reigned from 1533, when he was still an infant, to 1584. Staden refers to Ivan IV as *Grossfurst*, which corresponds to the Russian title *Velikii Kniaz*. Both terms literally mean Grand Prince; therefore I prefer that title to "Grand Duke," which is frequently used by historians. Actually Ivan's most significant title was "Tsar." He was the first of the Russian grand princes to assume officially (in 1547) the title of tsar, but it was some time before Russia's European neighbors acknowledged this.

[4] The Turkish Sultan was either Selim II, who ruled from 1566 to 1574, or Murad III, who ruled from 1574 to 1595.

Kazan was a Tatar city on the middle Volga. It was the capital of an independent khanate until 1552, when it was conquered by the Muscovites. Long before 1552, the Muscovites had held considerable political influence in the affairs of the khanate, and at times Kazan was little more than a Muscovite dependency.

Astrakhan was a town in the delta of the Volga and the capital of a khanate of the same name. It was conquered by Muscovite forces in 1556.

The Nogais were a tribe of Tatars who ranged the steppe land north of Astrakhan on both sides of the Volga.

Prince Mikhail Temriukovich Cherkasskii was in the service of

drously protected me in that country, and has rescued me unharmed from there—as my account truthfully reports —perhaps it is the will of God that I should reveal such conditions and opportunities to your Imperial Roman Majesty. So, according to your Imperial Roman Majesty's wishes and desires, I most humbly write of such things simply and most briefly. And if it should be necessary, I am prepared to make an oral and written report with detailed facts for the use and satisfaction of your Imperial Roman Majesty. When I was sent to Poland, the Polish King would have given much to have such a report from me. I had some reservations about writing one, however, and decided not to do it.[5]

I most humbly beg your Imperial Roman Majesty to accept this report graciously. I have honestly conceived it, and am exultant that my God has let me see your Imperial Roman Majesty with my own eyes. Now nothing troubles me. I have entrusted my soul to God alone, and my eyes and heart shall be prepared, for the rest of my

Ivan IV until 1571 or 1572, when he was executed. His father, Temriuk, was a Kabardinian prince who from 1557 to 1571 was allied with Ivan IV. In 1571 he transferred his allegiance to the Crimean Khan, with whom he remained until 1578, when he was again associated with the Muscovites. Temriuk's daughter (Mikhail's sister) was Ivan's second wife from 1561 until she died in 1569. Staden continually confuses the son with the father.

By "King of Poland," Staden usually means Stephen Bathory, who ruled Poland from 1576 to 1584. Before his election to the Polish throne, Bathory was the ruler of Transylvania and a vassal of the Turkish Sultan. This fact led many contemporaries, including Staden, to suppose that Bathory was in some way controlled by the Turks.

[5] Poland-Lithuania and Muscovy had been at war for some years. It is doubtful, however, that Staden's report would have added much to the knowledge of the Polish court, which was well supplied with Muscovite defectors.

life, to serve your Imperial Roman Majesty honorably, and in the way that you may choose.

I humbly request that your Imperial Roman Majesty keep this account, consider the project well, and carry it out—so that this good opportunity may not be lost. But I beg that my report not be copied and become generally known! The reason is this: the Grand Prince spares no expense to learn what is going on in other kingdoms and lands, and this is done with the utmost secrecy. He probably has connections, through merchants, with imperial, royal, and princely courts. The merchants are well supplied with money for bribery, which the Grand Prince wants used cautiously to protect him against unpleasant surprises. If he should learn of this project, he could fortify the seacoast I describe by building blockhouses at the river mouths and garrisoning them.

It might be said that I am doing this for money or some other reward; but I answer that I do it of my own free will for your Imperial Roman Majesty's pleasure, without expecting a reward. At the last judgment I shall feel indebted to God the Almighty and his Son, Jesus Christ, as well as the Holy Ghost, for the things God has permitted me to observe, which I have revealed and described.[6] Also, because I was born a subject of your Imperial Roman Majesty and because my kinsmen all live under this same highly praised and widely renowned government, I would be duty bound to report these things.

I hereby promise that when your Imperial Roman Majesty undertakes this Christian action and puts this

[6] Staden's religion is uncertain. He was probably born to a Catholic family, but may have become a Lutheran. His account is quite vague on this point, perhaps purposefully; Rudolf II was of course a Catholic.

4

proposal into practice, I, Heinrich von Staden, shall continue to serve you truly and nobly. Your Imperial Roman Majesty may perhaps learn from my report how I maintained myself in the service of the Grand Prince, who is the hereditary foe of all Christians, and an unspeakable tyrant. It is much more fitting that I serve your Imperial Roman Majesty, under whom my parents peacefully passed their days. I feel myself duty bound and obliged to serve you obediently in every way, chief of all Christians, in order that your leadership be not weakened and suppressed but extended. In order to be more trusted, I have signed this with my own hand: your Imperial Roman Majesty's most humble and obedient servant,

Heinrich von Staden
manu propria

II. *The Land and Government of Muscovy*

Described by Heinrich von Staden

A description of the Grand Prince in Muscovy, of the situation and the condition of the entire country, and how one lives and behaves there.

To the most eminent, all-powerful, unconquerable Roman Emperor, King of Bohemia and Hungary, Rudolf, our most noble lord. Hastily and briefly put to paper by me, Heinrich von Staden.

In Russia, at the court of the Grand Prince, in the city of Moscow, there were a number of *kniazi*—or princes—who had their own separate lands, cities, castles, and villages. To wit: Prince Vladimir Andreevich [Staritskii], Prince [Ivan] Dmitrievich Bel'skii, Prince Mikhail Vorotynskii, Prince Nikita Odoevskii, Prince Andrei Kurbskii, Prince Vasilii Temkin, Prince Petr Shuiskii, and many more princes; also Ivan Sheremetev and [Ivan Ivanovich] Turuntai[-Pronskii], as well as Aleksei Basmanov and his son Fedor, Ivan Mstislavskii, and many other leaders of high rank.[1]

[1] Prince Vladimir Andreevich Staritskii was the grandson of Vasilii III and the cousin of Ivan IV. Cliques opposed to Ivan IV sought twice, in 1553 and in 1567, to have Prince Vladimir replace Ivan on the throne. For years Ivan was suspicious of Prince Vladimir, and in 1569 had him poisoned.

Prince Ivan Dmitrievich Bel'skii was the leading boyar in the *zem-*

6

These men, in particular, have always warred against Russia's hereditary foe, the Crimean Khan. For this, five special leaders have been chosen from among them and others every year. Each leader has units from his own districts and cities.[2] The other princes and boyars[3] have troops with them from their pomestia and votchiny in accordance with the muster rolls. The fifth [regiment,

---

shchina (see note 19, p. 18). He died during the burning of Moscow by the Tatars in 1571.

Prince Mikhail Ivanovich Vorotynskii was the boyar and military commander who was perhaps most responsible for the Russian victory over the Crimean Tatars in 1572. He was executed in the following year.

Prince Nikita Romanovich Odoevskii was a boyar in the oprichnina. He frequently commanded Muscovite forces in the wars against the Crimean Tatars. He was executed in 1573.

Prince Andrei Mikhailovich Kurbskii was a boyar and *voevoda* who defected in 1564. He fought against Ivan IV with the Polish kings Sigismund August and Stephen Bathory until his death in 1583. Kurbskii had been closely trusted by Ivan, and his desertion probably influenced Ivan's decision to establish the oprichnina, which was started a few months after he left.

Temkin, Sheremetev, and Turuntai-Pronskii did not play especially prominent roles in the affairs Staden describes.

Prince Petr Ivanovich Shuiskii was a boyar and a member of an illustrious Russian family. He died in battle in 1564.

Aleksei Basmanov was a favorite of Ivan IV during the oprichnina period, and was an effective military leader and diplomat. He was nevertheless executed by Ivan for political reasons, perhaps in 1569, certainly no later than 1571. His son Fedor was reputedly a homosexual partner of Ivan IV. He was executed with his father.

[2] Some of the descendants of princes who had previously been sovereign, and who during Staden's time served the Grand Prince of Muscovy, maintained private military forces.

[3] A boyar had the highest administrative rank in Muscovite Russia. Supposedly the boyars as a group formed an advisory council for the grand princes and tsars; but this was not actually the case, since the sovereign had favorites and chose advisers from among the boyars and from outside their group.

which rode] in the midst of the other four, was the most distinguished, and therefore in this middle regiment there was a representative of the Grand Prince. When the enemy engaged them, the five regiments remained separate, each under its leader. When they advanced against the enemy, the first regiment went straight ahead; the second moved to the right; the third went to the left; the fourth regiment was the last or hindmost. Whichever regiment the enemy then attacked became the first. The *voevoda*[4] immediately took command of it or sent a captain. This was the vanguard. The other regiments remained in place, in battle order, and sent troops to assist the leader [of the vanguard] when it was necessary, so that the enemy could not break the battle formation from the flanks or the rear and the commander of the middle regiment would not be harmed or threatened.[5]

These military leaders and others like them took turns being governors, voevody, or commanders for two years in certain lands and city regions in the country. [There were more aristocrats than posts.] When the two years were up, they were changed. All the sins, burdens, outrages, oppression, and exploitation that they had inflicted upon the peasants and merchants and had forgotten were completed by their replacements. They had law books that should have been used to determine fair judgments, but they were not used.

---

[4] A *voevoda* (pl. *voevody*) was a military commander; he was also the highest provincial official or governor.

[5] Staden describes the deployment of forces for a major campaign. Less important campaigns involved fewer troops, and in such cases the two flank regiments were not used, leaving just three—the vanguard, the main force, and the rear guard.

8

Then there were boyars from great families who were judges in Moscow and held the entire government in their hands. One of these, or some other prince or boyar sat in every court of law and every other chancellery, and the clerk had to write down everything the judge ordered him to write.

When the Grand Prince was absent from Moscow, Ivan Petrovich Cheliadnin[6] was the chief boyar and judge. He alone was accustomed to judge fairly, and for that reason the common people liked him.

Nikita Funikov, Khoziain Iur'evich Tiutin, and the clerk Grigorii Lokurov were in the State Treasury. They received all the money from the other chancelleries—the country's income—and gave from the Treasury to each, according to favor. They extracted the third penny from the common folk in every way, and filled their own pockets well. Yet they brought the accounts to the Grand Prince in full order.

Nikita Romanovich was in charge of the *podkletnye sela*. Those are the estates belonging to the court household. What he did there was not questioned, because he was the Grand Prince's brother-in-law.

Putilo Mikhailovich and Vasilii Stepanovich were in the Land Chancellery. These two filled their own pockets well, for although they were ordered simply to assign estates, they collected money for half of them, and those who had nothing to give received nothing.

Ivan Grigor'evich [Vyrodkov] was in the Military Chancellery. The princes and boyars who paid money at

---

[6] Ivan Petrovich Cheliadnin was a boyar and a member of an old Muscovite family. He remained in the zemshchina and governed Moscow when the oprichnina was established. In 1567 or 1568, he was executed without trial for supposedly conspiring with the Poles.

this chancellery were not put on the muster rolls, and those who could not pay had to go [on campaign] even if they could appear for muster with nothing more than a staff. All Polish affairs were dealt with in this chancellery.

Ivan Bulgakov was in the Court Treasury. Money from other cities and districts was paid and weighed here, one-fiftieth of it always going astray before being reckoned. And when the money was paid out by the chancellery, one-tenth was always missing.

Grigorii Shapkin was in the Criminal Affairs Chancellery. When someone was arrested for murder anywhere in the country—in districts, cities, villages, or on the highways—and could pay off, he was egged on [by members of the chancellery] and forced to accuse a merchant or a rich peasant of having helped him murder. The great men got money in this way.

Ivan Dolgorukii and Ivan Miatlev sat in the lower law court or *Zemskii Dvor*.[7] All those who were found drunk at night in the streets were seized and brought before the law here. The fine was ten *altin*, which is equal to thirty *mariagroschen* or Polish *groschen*; and whenever beer, mead, or brandy was found in illegal taverns, it was taken and brought to this court. [The culprit] then had to pay the set fine of two rubles, which is six talers, and he was then publicly whipped in the marketplace with a lash. There were many *prikazchiki*[8] or officials who supervised this. They could right a wrong in the street before a person was brought to this court, and

---

[7] The *Zemskii Dvor*, the lower law court, was responsible for civil suits, misdemeanors, and the maintenance of order in Moscow.

[8] *Prikazchiki* (sing. *prikazchik*) were functionaries in *prikazi*—governmental chancelleries.

on the other hand, could also wrong a right. If these officials did not like some merchant or tradesman and knew he had money, a young tramp would be sent to his house carrying a small bottle of brandy in his blouse. The officials would immediately appear with jurors and seize the boy and the man and woman of the house, together with the servant and maid. The man could not spare his purse then, if he wanted to keep his skin whole.

There were many *nedel'shchiki*[9] whom one could send, for a sum determined by distance, to bring a person before the law from anywhere in the country. The accused was assigned a date for appearance [in court] according to whether he lived nearby or far away. The nedel'shchik therefore, when he first arrived at a place, took along two or three witnesses from the nearest customshouse outside of the estates or regions, and threw a summons into the house or court of the accused. This happened up to three times. If the accused gave money, he was acquitted even if he was guilty. If he did not come, the accuser could then arrest and bind him and have him beaten publicly in the marketplace until he paid. The accuser was also permitted, if he wished, to make the accused a serf, and the accused was not shown mercy until he paid with interest. Otherwise he had to spend the rest of his life pulling a hand mill. Many evil fellows were incited to accuse a rich merchant or a rich peasant in the country falsely, but correct [observance of] legal procedure was necessary. These fellows got money in this way.

Customarily all letters were ordered dispatched by the *Iamskaia Izba*—or Post Chancellery. The employees often let them accumulate and then sent them off all at

[9] *Nedel'shchiki* (sing. *nedel'shchik*) were petty officials of the law courts.

once. They then drew up a full account of how many horses were [supposedly] rented, and kept the money that should have gone to the Treasury.

In the chancellery where all petitions were read, approved, and signed by the Grand Prince, those who had money received their signed petitions, and the townsman or commoner who had no money could get no information until he gave some. Only then was his petition read and signed. *Ruka ruku moet*, one hand washes the other.

In the Kazan and Astrakhan Chancelleries, and [in the corresponding] empires, they have filled their purses well, likewise in the surrounding ulus [nomad villages] of the Lugovye and Nagornye Cheremisians.[10]

At the Chancellery for Ryazan they also behaved very unscrupulously at that time. At present, however, this is forbidden, because the Crimean Khan has dealt with this land [Ryazan] as the Grand Prince has dealt with Livonia.[11]

---

[10] Lugovye and Nagornye Cheremisians were Finnish people who lived in the forests north of Kazan between the Volga and Kama rivers. They were divided into two groups: the plains (lugovye) and the hill (nagornye) Cheremisians.

[11] Livonia, an area on the eastern Baltic, was conquered by a crusading order of German knights in the thirteenth century. The knights developed estates in the land, and German merchants built flourishing commercial cities that helped bring east-European and especially Russian products to the West. By the middle of the sixteenth century, Livonia, legally part of the Holy Roman Empire, was divided into towns, bishoprics, and lands held by the Livonian Order of Knights. Hence authority was fragmented, and the resultant mutual animosity precluded any united effort to defend the country from the Muscovites. Ivan IV invaded in 1558, and in the early 1560's the Livonian Order ceased to exist, its land being divided among the Russians, the Poles and Lithuanians, the Swedes, and the Danish Duke Magnus. The war for control of Livonia continued until 1581, when the Russians were driven out and only the Poles, Danes, and Swedes remained.

Andrei Vasilievich sat in the Chancellery for Ambassadors. All German and Tatar affairs were dealt with here, and the income from Karelia was received. Every day there were interpreters from many different nations here. These interpreters also had estates and annual allowances. The same tricks were played here as at the other chancelleries.

Ivan Tarasovich Soimonov, and one clerk, sat at the *iamme*, or the court where all the foreigners received their daily money allowance. When a foreigner did not pick up his mead or money allowance for ten, twenty, or thirty days, one-tenth was always withheld when he wanted to receive it.

Each foreigner had a chit so artfully made that no one could forge additions without their being noticed. Mead was taken from the cellars by those who were assigned that task. They measured out the mead in the cellar as they wished, and then brought it out. It was then poured into the casks of the foreigner. If he wanted to take it, good; if not, he got nothing. They brewed good and poorer mead, and by doing this they saved one-third of the honey. If a foreigner gave these fellows a present, he could go into the cellar and have all the barrels tapped. [He then could decide] which one tasted best, and have it tapped and receive his full measure. When a foreigner died or was killed, these fellows [still] brought everything into full account for an entire year [and kept or sold the rest of his ration].

In brief, these were the foremost chancelleries. The others operated in the same way.

The money income of the country was apportioned so that each chancellery had money and jurisdiction over the corresponding land [from which the money was de-rived]. Money was not transferred from a chancellery. One chancellery would get from another a note or memorandum, which had to be signed by the clerk. They were pasted together with glue and rolled up.[12]

There were two doormen at every chancellery or law court. They opened the doors for those who gave money. The doors remained closed to those who had nothing to give, and if a person tried to force his way in, he was struck hard on the head with a stick two-and-a-half feet long. No one was spared. The doorman would open the door for a man who had no money, if he knocked and said, "Gospodi Iisuse Khriste, syne Bozhii, pomilui nas greshnykh." [Lord Jesus Christ, have mercy on us sinners.] He then went inside and repeatedly entreated the princes, boyars, or clerks. If he was not courageous then one of them beat or pushed him with his staff and said, "Nedosug; podozhdi!"—[that is] "I don't have time; wait!" Many a man was detained until he died. Every prince, boyar, and clerk has a staff with him at all times in the chancelleries and churches.

In every chancellery, all affairs large and small were written in books once a year; and in every chancellery plum or cherry stones were used for counting.

In all chancelleries there were between twenty and fifty underclerks, or *pod'iachie*. They made clean copies of all documents. A clerk would take a document in his left hand and write his name in small letters under the date. He then would turn the document over and write in every place where it was glued, so that half of the letters were on each end of each paper. If the glue did not

[12] The chancelleries had jurisdiction over tax collecting; often this involved just specific taxes. The Treasury also collected taxes. Government finances were chaotic.

hold, no one could forge the document or write more into it. After this, the document was bound. Then the clerk wrote outside on the top of the first leaf of those documents that remained in the country, "Ivan Vasilievich, Tsar and Grand Prince of all Russia." [He wrote] the name of the Grand Prince freehand in large letters so everyone could read it. An inkpot with quills stood on the desk in front of the clerk. All the pod'iachie—or underclerks—held their inkpots, quills, and paper in their left hands, and leaning on their laps, wrote clean copies of the documents.

In the summer a number of boys or youths went around with wooden cups and stone jugs in which ice lay. When a person was thirsty, he could drink one, two, or three times for a Bohemian penny. Some, who went into all the chancelleries, had a drink to sell called *sladkii mors*. It was prepared like this: the Russians took some water from a fresh-flowing stream, then placed some juniper berries in the water, which thereupon became bitter. Then they took honey and mixed it with the water and strained [the mixture] through a hair sack, making it as sweet as one wished, and one paid for it accordingly.

When, in the countryside or in any city of Muscovy, a person could not get justice, he went to these or similar chancelleries.

When two parties came together [in a legal dispute] and the plaintiff swore an oath, winning the case, the accused was able, before paying, to challenge the plaintiff to combat to test the oath.[13] There were many fighters in Moscow who would fight on anyone's behalf for money.

[13] The oath consisted of swearing that something or other was true and then kissing the cross. If this was insufficient, a case could be decided in a trial by combat.

Anyone who had won a case with an oath and whose opponent [in the case] was not satisfied, had to fight his opponent in personal combat. He also had the right to hire a fighter in his stead. It was always found, therefore, that the man who was in the right and had sworn an oath was not in the right if the other party had more money. Even if the latter was in the wrong, he was still found right and the right was found wrong. When the professional fighters fought, the one who had received the most money from the other fell to the ground before his opponent in full armor and said: "Vinovat, kazni"—that is, "I am guilty."[14] With these words the one in the wrong won and the one in the right lost, for the wrong had more money than the right.

When a person received his signed document from these or other chancelleries, [he took it to] Ivan Viskovatyi[15] who had the seal. Viskovatyi was very proud, and one could be happy to get the signed document back from him within a month. He would have been glad to see the Crimean Khan take Russia, and was therefore well-disposed to all Tatars, and assisted them, but he was very hostile to Christians [i.e., Europeans like Staden].

In addition to these [princes and boyars of high rank] there were princes and boyars of low rank. They were assigned as functionaries in the podkletnye sela, large settlements belonging to the court [of the Grand Prince]. The peasants and merchants are accustomed to obey them, according to the wishes of the princes and boyars.

---

[14] The Russian actually reads "I am guilty; execute me."

[15] Ivan Mikhailovich Viskovatyi was a leading official in the zemshchina. For years he was in charge of the Chancellery for Ambassadors. He was a boyar and Keeper of the Seal from 1561 to 1570 or 1571, when he was executed.

If a person wanted to complain to the Grand Prince, [the princes and boyars] were diligent in seeing that he was thrown into prison. If he had money, he could go free. If he had none, he remained sitting in prison until his hair grew from his head to his navel.

All these princes, great ruling boyars, clerks, under-clerks, functionaries, and all authorities were dependent on one another and were interlaced like the links of a chain.

When one of these or the like sinned so awfully that he was condemned to death, the metropolitan[16] had the power to take him from the jailer and set him free. And if one had robbed, murdered, or stolen, and lived with the money and goods in a monastery, he was as free in the monastery as in heaven, even if he had stolen the money from the Grand Prince's Treasury, or robbed on the road what belonged to the Treasury. In brief, all ec-clesiastical and secular lords who won their property un-justly say facetiously, "Bog dal,"—i.e., *deus dedit*. God has given it. They have ruled in the same way under all the earlier, now deceased, grand princes.

A number [of the deceased grand princes] began the oprichnina action but were unable to accomplish any-thing.[17] The present Grand Prince likewise could not ac-complish anything until he married the daughter of Prince Mikhail Temriukovich, from the Circassian re-gion.[18] She advised the Grand Prince to choose five hun-

[16] The metropolitan was the highest ecclesiastical official in Mus-covy until the establishment of the patriarchate in 1590.

[17] They attempted administrative reforms. No prince before Ivan IV created an institution like the oprichnina. (The oprichnina is de-scribed in the Introduction.)

[18] Ivan married Maria, daughter of Prince Temriuk Cherkasskii, in 1561. Mikhail was her brother. Staden has again confused Mikhail with his father, Temriuk.

dred harquebusiers from among his people and gen-
erously provide them with clothes and money. They
were to ride with him daily and guard him day and
night. Ivan Vasilievich, Grand Prince of all Russia,
thereupon undertook this and chose from his own and
foreign nations a hand-picked order, thus creating the
oprichnina and the *zemshchina*.[19]

The oprichnina was [composed of] his people; the
zemshchina, of the ordinary people. The Grand Prince
thus began to inspect one city and region after another.
And those who, according to the military muster rolls,
had not served [the Grand Prince's] forefathers by
fighting the enemy with their votchiny were deprived of
their estates, which were given to those in the oprichnina.

The princes and boyars who were taken into the
oprichnina were ranked not according to riches but according to birth. They then took an oath not to have anything to do with the *zemskie* people or form any friendships with them. Those in the oprichnina also had to
wear black clothes and hats; and in their quivers, where
they put their arrows, they carried some kind of brushes
or brooms tied on the ends of sticks. The *oprichniki*[20]
were recognized in this way.

Because of insurrection [in Moscow in December
1564], the Grand Prince left Moscow for Aleksandrova
Sloboda, a two-day trip. He placed guards in this slo-

[19] The *zemshchina* was the area of the Muscovite realm that was not
taken into the oprichnina. It was governed as before, but its inhabitants
were subjected to the arbitrariness of persons from the more powerful
oprichnina. The inhabitants of the zemshchina were called the *zemskie*
people. The oprichnina did not begin in precisely the way Staden describes.

[20] *Oprichniki* (sing. *oprichnik*) were members of the oprichnina,
but not the commoners who merely dwelled in oprichnina territory.

boda, and had any nobles that he wanted called to him from Moscow and other cities.[21]

The Grand Prince sent an order to the zemskie people saying that they must judge justly: "Sudite pravedno, nashi vinovaty ne byli by"—that is, "Judge justly, ours [the oprichniki] shall not be in the wrong."[22] Because of this order, the zemskie people became despondent. A person from the oprichnina could accuse someone from the zemshchina of owing him a sum of money. And even if the oprichnik had never known nor seen the accused from the zemshchina, the latter had to pay him immediately or he was publicly beaten in the marketplace with knouts or cudgels every day until he paid. No one was spared in this, neither clerics nor laymen. The oprichniki did a number of indescribable things to the zemskie people to get all their money and property.... And the [professional] fighters were beaten until they were dead yet alive, and they were no longer allowed to be fighters.[23]

The Grand Prince arrived in Moscow from Aleksandrova Sloboda and murdered one of the chief men of the zemshchina, Ivan Petrovich Cheliadnin. In the Grand Prince's absence from Moscow, this man was the chief

[21] Aleksandrova Sloboda was a town and fortress northeast of Moscow in the vicinity of Pereyaslavl-Zalesski. After it ceased to be a village, it was still called a "sloboda," although that term generally referred to a large village or settlement. In the sixteenth century it was a royal residence, and during the oprichnina period it assumed great importance as the residence and headquarters of Ivan. (See illustration p. 20.)

[22] The Russian literally reads "Judge justly, ours must not be held guilty."

[23] *Hie galt kein*— A break in the text. Epstein supposed the meaning to be that judicial duels no longer applied when the plaintiff was an oprichnik and the accused a zemskii person.

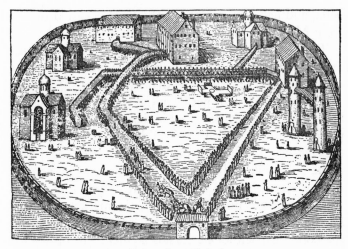

Aleksandrova Sloboda

boyar and judge. He willingly helped the poor people
find justice quickly, and for a number of years he was
governor and commander in Livonia—at Dorpat and at
Polotsk. As long as he was commander at Dorpat in
Livonia, the Germans did not have to worry that the
Grand Prince would have them led into Russia from
Narva, Fellin [Vilyandi], and Dorpat [Tartu].[24]

Prince Andrei Kurbskii was governor and commander
after him. When [Kurbskii] became aware of the
oprichnina business, he rode off to King Sigismund August in Poland, leaving behind his wife and children.[25]
In his place came the boyar Mikhail Morozov. He so

[24] The removal of large numbers of people from a conquered area
into the central regions of Muscovy was an old Muscovite practice.
The rulers of such populations were thus removed from their bases of
power. I assume that some merchants and artisans were also deported
because of the contributions they could make to the economy of the
central regions.

[25] Sigismund August was King of Poland from 1548 to 1572. He
was the last Jagiello to occupy the Polish throne.

20

slandered the Livonians to the Grand Prince that the
Grand Prince had all the Germans, together with their
wives and children, at Dorpat, Fellin, and Narva led
from Livonia into his country to the four cities of Kostroma, Vladimir, Uglich, and Kassma [Kazan or Kashin?].

Afterward [Cheliadnin] was summoned to Moscow.
In Moscow he was killed and thrown into a filthy pit
near the Neglinna river. The Grand Prince then went
with his oprichniki and burned all the votchiny in the
country belonging to this Ivan Petrovich. The villages
were burned with their churches and everything that was
in them, icons and church ornaments. Women and girls
were stripped naked and forced in that state to catch
chickens in the fields. The oprichniki caused great misery
in the country, and many people were secretly murdered.

This was too much for the zemskie people. They be-
gan to confer, and they decided to elect as grand prince
Vladimir Andreevich [Staritskii], whose daughter Duke
Magnus[26] had [married], and to kill and extirpate the
Grand Prince and all his oprichniki. To this effect they
signed an agreement [in 1567 or 1568].

The chief men and princes in the zemshchina were
these: Prince Vladimir Andreevich [Staritskii], Prince
Ivan Dmitrievich Bel'skii, Nikita Romanovich,[27] and
Metropolitan Philip with his bishops of Kazan, Astra-

---

[26] Magnus, Prince of Denmark and Duke of Holstein, was the
brother of the Danish king, Frederick II. In 1561, as Livonia was dis-
integrating, Magnus assumed control of the Bishopric of Ösel (Saare)
and later established friendly relations with Ivan IV, who named him
"King of Livonia" in 1570. As such, he was expected to conquer the
rest of Livonia and rule it as Ivan's vassal. In this manner Ivan hoped
to win over the Livonian nobility, who preferred a German (or at
least a Dane) to a Russian sovereign. The plan was unsuccessful.

[27] Nikita Romanovich was a boyar and military commander. His
sister Anastasia was Ivan's first wife, and his grandson, Mikhail, was
the first Romanov tsar.

khan, Ryazan, Vladimir, Vologda, Rostov, Suzdal, Tver, Polotsk, Great Novgorod, Nizhni Novgorod, Pskov, and Dorpat in Livonia. It can be assumed that [Metropolitan Philip] will also establish a bishop in Riga. All these bishops had to appear personally in Moscow every year at the procession of the metropolitan on Palm Sunday; then [behind them in the procession] came all monks and priests from monasteries, and the *sobornye*—that is, those who are members of the council.

Briefly, with the Grand Prince in the oprichnina were Prince Afanasii Viazemskii, Maliuta Skuratov,[28] and Aleksei Basmanov and his son Fedor.

The Grand Prince set out with large cannons, knowing nothing of the agreement [uniting the zemskie people under Prince Vladimir], and advanced to the Lithuanian border at Porkhov. His plan was to capture the city of Vilna in Lithuania, and if not that, Riga in Livonia.[29]

First, the Bloody Savage had advanced to Riga in Livonia, intending to take the city through kindness or trickery.[30] When that failed, he tried to take the city by force. Then several thousand Poles fell outside Riga. When the Grand Prince heard of this, he sent for

[28] Prince Afanasii Ivanovich Viazemskii participated in the organization of the oprichnina, and was one of its most prominent members. He was executed after the Novgorod campaign.

Maliuta Skuratov was an oprichnik who died in battle in 1572.

[29] Riga was the largest and most important commercial city in Livonia. After the disintegration of the Livonian Order in the early 1560's, Riga strove to continue as an independent city; but it finally had to submit to the Poles. It was not conquered by the Russians during the Livonian war.

[30] It is unclear who Staden calls the Bloody Savage (*der Rotewilde*). Epstein suggests that it is a corruption of the name Radziwill. Staden confused Nicholas Radziwill, the Palatine of Vilna, with Jan Chodkiewicz, the Polish commander in Livonia. In 1567 Chodkiewicz led a Polish force against Livonia.

22

the Master [of the Livonian Order], Wilhelm Fürstenberg,[31] and had him brought before him. The Grand
Prince sat in his court array with his eldest son. The
oprichniki stood in the hall facing the Grand Prince from
the right. The zemskie leaders faced him from the left.
Wilhelm Fürstenberg stood in ceremonial attire before
the Grand Prince. I stood not far from Wilhelm Fürstenberg and the interpreter, Caspar von Wittenberg, in
order to hear if the interpreter translated correctly.

The Grand Prince then began to speak. "Former Master of Livonia! We want to favor you and set you up in
Livonia again. You must only promise us, and seal [the
promise] with an oath, that you will also seize the rest
[of Livonia]—Reval [Tallinn], the Bishopric of Riga,
Kurland, and everything that belonged to your former
government. After you, the young Master Wilhelm Kettler shall rule in our patrimony up to the coast of the
Baltic." Wilhelm Fürstenberg answered the Grand
Prince, saying, "I have never heard or known that Livonia was your patrimony up to the coast of the Baltic."
The Grand Prince said, "Then have you also [not] seen
fire, sword, murder, and killing, and have you not seen
how you and others have been led captive from Livonia?
So answer, what will you do?" Wilhelm Fürstenberg
then answered, "I have sworn an oath to the Roman Empire and I will live and die by it."[32] The Grand Prince

[31] Wilhelm von Fürstenberg, the second-last Master of the Livonian
Order of Knights (1557–1559), was captured by Russian forces when
they took the Livonian fortress of Fellin in 1560. In captivity, he was
settled in the town of Lyubim, northeast of Moscow. Nothing is known
of him after 1566 although in his autobiography Staden refers to
"the deceased Master Wilhelm Fürstenberg," indicating that he was
dead before Staden left Russia (probably in 1576).

[32] Livonia was legally a part of the Holy Roman Empire.

became angry at this, and Wilhelm Fürstenberg was sent back to Lyubim. Otherwise he would have set off with the Grand Prince for Riga, and all Germans would have been granted money and clothes. [Now] all that was set aside. Thereupon Duke Magnus was thought of. The honor he gained is well known.

Prince Vladimir Andreevich [Staritskii] revealed the compact to the Grand Prince, and revealed everything that the zemskie people had planned and prepared. The Grand Prince then started a rumor that he did not want to advance to Lithuania or to Riga, but that he wanted to tour and inspect his patrimonial lands. He then returned by post road to Aleksandrova Sloboda, and had someone write down [the names of] those zemskie leaders whom he wanted slaughtered, killed, and executed first.

There was a guard post called Karinskii three versts south of the sloboda on the Moscow road. All those in the sloboda with the Grand Prince could not leave, nor could anyone enter from outside without a *pamiat'*—a memorandum, that is—as identification. All the disloyal servants of the zemskie leaders knew of this, and when one of them came to the guard and said, "U menia est' dela gospodarskie"—that is, "I have business with the Grand Prince or the boyars"[33]—the guard immediately accompanied him to the chancellery in the sloboda, where everything he said about his master was believed.

The Grand Prince continued to have one [zemskii] leader after another seized and killed as it came into his head, one this way, another that way.

Metropolitan Philip could remain silent about this

---

[33] The Russian actually reads "I have government business."

business no longer, and spoke affably to the Grand Prince saying that he ought to live and rule as his forefathers had. The good metropolitan fell into disgrace with these words, and he had to lie in very large iron chains until he died. The Grand Prince then chose a metropolitan according to his wishes.[34]

After that the Grand Prince set out from Aleksandrova Sloboda with all his oprichniki. Every city, road, and monastery from the sloboda to Livonia was occupied by oprichnina guards, as though it were done because of plague, so that one city or monastery could learn of nothing from another.

The oprichniki came to the *iam*—or post station—at Chernaya and began to plunder. The places where the Grand Prince spent the night were set afire and were burned down the next morning.

All those who came from Moscow to the guard post and wanted to go to the camp of [Ivan's] own handpicked people, whether they were princes or boyars or their servants, were seized by the guards, bound, and immediately killed. Some were stripped naked in front of the Grand Prince and rolled around in the snow until they died. The same thing happened to those who wanted to leave the camp for Moscow and were caught by the guards.

The Grand Prince then arrived at the city of Tver and had everything plundered, even churches and monasteries. And he had all the prisoners killed, likewise his own people who had befriended or married foreigners.

[34] Kirill became metropolitan in 1568. Metropolitan Philip did not speak "affably" to Ivan about the oprichnina; in a sermon, he sharply criticized the tsar for his behavior. He was later strangled at Ivan's command.

All the bodies had their legs cut off, because of the ice, and were then stuck under the ice of the Volga River.[35] The same occurred in the city of Torzhok. Neither church nor monastery was spared here.

The Grand Prince arrived again outside the city of Great Novgorod.[36] He settled down three furlongs from the city and sent in an army commander with his retinue. He was to spy and reconnoiter. The rumor was that the Grand Prince wanted to march to Livonia. Then the Grand Prince moved into Great Novgorod, into the bishop's palace, and took everything belonging to the bishop. He took the largest bells and whatever he wanted from the churches. The Grand Prince thus left the city alone. He ordered the merchants to buy and sell and to ask a just price from his soldiers, the oprichniki. Every day he arose and moved to another monastery. He indulged his wantonness and had monks tortured, and many of them were killed. There are three hundred monasteries inside and outside the city and not one of these was spared. Then the pillage of the city began. And every morning when the Grand Prince came to the city from his camp, the chief person of the city had to ride to him so that he could learn what occurred in the city during the night.

[35] Why their legs were cut off is uncertain.

[36] Great Novgorod, located on the Volkhov River in the northwest part of the country, was the second-largest city of Russia. It was the major center of Russia's trade with the West, and for centuries had been an independent republic. In the 1470's Novgorod was deprived of its independence by Ivan III, and it was integrated into the expanding Muscovite empire. Antipathy for Moscow's domination, however, remained in some quarters of the city's ruling class. Ivan IV ravaged Novgorod in 1570, when the city's leaders conspired with Sigismund August of Poland-Lithuania and their antipathy seemed to be turning into open treason.

This distress and misery continued in the city for six weeks without interruption [in January and February, 1570]. Every shop and room where money or property were thought to be was sealed. Every day the Grand Prince could also be found in the torture chamber in person. Nothing might remain in the monasteries and the city. Everything that the soldiers could not carry off was thrown into the water or burned. If one of the zemskie people retrieved anything from the water, he was hanged.

All foreign prisoners, most of whom were Poles, were then killed along with their wives and children, as well as [Ivan's] people who had married foreigners. All high buildings were torn down and all beautiful doors, steps, and windows chopped up. Several thousand daughters of the inhabitants were carried off by the oprichniki. A number of zemskie people dressed themselves like oprichniki and caused great mischief and damage. They were hunted down and killed.

The Grand Prince then moved on to Pskov,[37] and began a similar operation. He sent captains and soldiers to Narva and Lake Ladoga on the Swedish border, and had the property of his Russians taken and destroyed. [The Russians] were thrown into the water, and a number were burned. So many thousand clerics and laymen were killed on this day; such a thing had never before been heard of in Russia.

The Grand Prince had half of this city [Pskov] plundered until he came to the house of Mikula. This Mikula is a fine fellow and lives alone in his house in the city of

[37] Pskov was a commercial city-republic in northwestern Russia. It retained its independence until 1510, when it was absorbed by the Muscovite empire.

Pskov without wife or children. He has many animals that spend the entire winter in the muck of the court under open sky. They certainly grow and prosper. He is rich because of them, and he prophesies the future for the Russians. The Grand Prince went to him in his house. Mikula said to the Grand Prince, "It is enough. Return home!" The Grand Prince obeyed this Mikula and left Pskov for Aleksandrova Sloboda with all the money and property and many large bells.[38] He immediately had a stone church built in the sloboda, and he had the cash put there. A door that he had taken from the church in Great Novgorod was put on this church. The door was cast with historical figures. The bells were hung in the church.

After this, the Grand Prince, in public, put poison into the drink of Prince Vladimir Andreevich [Staritskii] and had [his] womenfolk stripped naked and shamefully shot by the harquebusiers. Of [Prince Vladimir's] boyars or princes, none remained.[39]

The Grand Prince left Aleksandrova Sloboda again for Moscow, and had all the authorities and commanders of the zemshchina and all clerks arrested.

Ivan Viskovatyi had the seal in the zemshchina, Nikita Funikov was treasurer, Ivan Bulgakov was in the Court Treasury. The Grand Prince murdered about 130 leaders here, all of whom had judged and ruled throughout the country. Ivan Viskovatyi first had his nose and ears cut off, and then his hands. Nikita Funikov had his arms bound to poles in the marketplace, and hot water was poured on him and he was thus scalded.

[38] It seems unlikely that this Mikula could have persuaded Ivan to leave; but different versions of the story are told in other sources.

[39] Prince Vladimir was actually executed in January 1569, before the Novgorod expedition.

It was also a period of great famine, when one man killed another for a crust of bread. In the podkletnye sela of the court, the Grand Prince had many thousand ricks of unthreshed grain in straw, which belonged to the household, but he would not sell them to his subjects; thus many thousand people died in the country and were eaten by dogs.

God the Almighty sent a great plague with this [1570–71]. Whatever court or house the pestilence visited was immediately nailed up, and if a person died within, he had to be buried there. Many died of hunger in their own courts and houses. Throughout the country, all cities, monasteries, settlements, and villages, as well as all the roads and highways, were guarded so that a person could not pass from one to another. And if a person were caught by the guard, he was immediately thrown into the fire that was next to the guard [post] along with everything he had with him—wagon, saddle, bridle. Here and there in the country, many thousand people who had died of the pestilence were eaten by dogs. When the plague got the upper hand, large pits were dug around the city of Moscow, and the dead were thrown in them without coffins, two hundred, three hundred, four hundred, five hundred in a pile. Along the highways in Muscovy special churches were built where prayers were said daily that God would ward off the plague.

An elephant had been given to the Grand Prince along with an Arab who looked after it. This Arab received a lot of money in Moscow, and this was noted by the Russian *brazhniki*—who were vagabonds and drunkards that played dice and gambled in the illegal taverns. They secretly murdered the Arab's wife for money. This Arab and his elephant were accused by the Russians of having brought on the plague, which had never before been thought of in Moscow.[40] The Arab and his elephant were then sent in disgrace to the town of Gorodets. The Arab died, and the Grand Prince sent a boyar who was instructed to kill the elephant with the help of the townsmen and the [peasants of the] surrounding *sokhi*.[41] The elephant stood in a shed with a palisade around it, not far from where the Arab lay buried. The elephant broke through and lay on the grave. He was then killed, and afterward his tusks were broken off and taken to the Grand Prince as evidence that he was dead.

In accordance with their oath, the oprichniki were not permitted to say a single word to those in the zemshchina, nor marry persons from the zemshchina; and if the father and mother of a person in the oprichnina lived in the zemshchina, that person was not allowed to go to them ever again.

The Grand Prince divided the city of Moscow into two parts. He took quite a small part [for himself], and left the city and the palace [the Kremlin] to the zemskie people. And as soon as the Grand Prince took a city or region of the country into the oprichnina, he immediately took one or two streets from the surrounding suburbs [of Moscow] into the oprichnina. Thus, the leaders and common people of the zemshchina diminished, and the Grand Prince became strong in the expanding oprichnina.

Those princes or boyars who were not included in the

[40] Staden errs; plagues were not at all uncommon in Moscow.

[41] *Sokhi* (sing. *sokha*) were areas in Muscovy established for purposes of taxation, and used until the middle of the seventeenth century. In the countryside, a sokha generally encompassed from twelve to sixteen thousand acres, and in the city, a certain number of houses. The estates and houses of those who served the tsar were not part of the sokhi.

muster rolls of the oprichnina were listed in a register. The register was sent to Prince [Ivan] Dmitrievich Bel'-skii and the other leaders of the zemshchina so that they would receive estates in other regions to replace their [confiscated] votchiny. This seldom occurred. When it did occur and the Grand Prince mustered a region and the oprichniki took the votchiny of the zemskie people, they took everything they found on the estates and let the zemskie people take nothing away that the oprichniki desired.

A small stream called the Neglinna flows through Moscow, one foot broad and deep [*ein schuch hoch und breit*]. This stream was the boundary between the op-richnina and the zemshchina. The Grand Prince had a large court built on this stream, the likes of which was never seen in Russia. This court cost the whole country so much that the zemskie people wished it would burn down. The Grand Prince learned of this and told his oprichniki that he would give the zemskie people such a fire that they would not soon be able to put it out. And he gave the oprichniki the liberty to treat the zemskie people badly in every way.

In the country many persons formed bands and rode out as though they were oprichniki. On the highways they murdered everyone they encountered. They pil-laged many unfortified settlements and cities, killing the people and burning the houses. They also acquired a lot of money that was being sent from other cities to Mos-cow, which would have gone into the Treasury. This situation was not looked after.

A lieutenant of the King of Poland, Aleksandr Polu-benski, from Livonia, set out with eight hundred Poles disguised as oprichniki. With him, however, were three boyars[42] who had deserted the Grand Prince: Mark Sary-khozin, his brother Anisim, and Timofei Teterin, who had been a harquebusier captain with the Grand Prince in Russia. Teterin feared the displeasure of the Grand Prince, and took vows in a monastery and came before the King [of Poland] hooded [like a monk]. The lieutenant then went to Izborsk [a fortified town near Pskov] and said to the guard at the gate, "Open up, I come from the oprichnina!" The gate was opened immediately. The Poles thus surprised Izborsk. They held it not longer than fourteen days, and surrendered it again to the Russian oprichniki. The Poles [who surrendered] were favored with estates and peasants. Those who wanted to keep Izborsk were killed.

In Livonia, the Russians at Fellin, Tarvast [Mustla], and Marienburg [Aluksne], wanted to surrender to the Poles. The Grand Prince learned of this and had all the chief clerks and authorities in these cities and castles beheaded. The heads were sent in sacks to Moscow as evidence.

The Grand Prince thereupon sent an order to all frontier posts and cities: no one claiming to be from the oprichnina should be admitted.

Many set out from the oprichnina and went to the coast of the White Sea[43] with falsified instructions, and began to requisition the daughters of all the rich merchants and peasants in unfortified settlements, pretending that the Grand Prince wanted them in Moscow. If a peasant or merchant gave money, his daughter was ex-

---

[42] Staden often used the title "boyar" when the person named was not of that rank. It seems that for Staden a boyar was merely a person who had some prominence.

[43] *Westsehe.* By this term Staden meant the White Sea proper as well as the waters off the north shore of the Kola peninsula.

cluded from the list as though she were not pretty, and those who were plain had to be listed as pretty. In this way they got money.

If the oprichniki, in the countryside where their farms and estates bordered the zemshchina, wanted a field or woods, meadow or pond, they dug two ditches. The first was four yards long and wide and [the land] up to it belonged in the oprichnina; the other was two yards long and wide and [the land] up to it was the zemshchina's.

All the peasants in the country have the right to move [off the estates they are living on] on St. George's Day in the winter [November 26]. They belong to whom they want.[44] Those who would not pass voluntarily from the zemshchina to the oprichnina were seized by force, regardless of the date. With that, their houses were taken away and burned.

Thus, many thousand rich merchants and many boyars and rich wholesalers from the zemshchina who did not serve in war, together with their votchiny, wives, and children, and everything they owned, went to oprichniki whom they knew.[45] They sold them their votchiny thinking they would thus be free of the other oprichniki. And when the oprichniki had plundered them they said, "We cannot keep you any longer. You know that we may not have relations with those in the zemshchina, and it is also against our oath. Go back to where you came from." And they had to thank God that they escaped without a beating.

The oprichniki ransacked the entire countryside and all the cities and villages of the zemshchina, although

[44] The peasants were still *legally* free to choose new masters if they paid their debts to their former lords.
[45] Obviously they couldn't have taken the lands, but they probably took everything movable on the votchiny.

33

the Grand Prince had not given them permission to do that. They drew up instructions themselves, as though the Grand Prince had ordered them to kill this or that merchant or noble—if he was thought to have money—along with his wife and children, and to take his money and property to the Grand Prince's Treasury. In the zemshchina, they thus committed many murders and assassinations, which are beyond description. Many who did not want to murder came to a place where they thought there was money, and seized the people and tortured them so long and so severely that they got all the cash and everything they wanted. The commoners in the oprichnina, the townsmen and peasants and all their servants, and the menials and maids brought suits against the zemskie people to get their money. I will not say what the servants, maids, and boys of the [oprichnina] princes and nobles permitted themselves. In the letter of the law everything is legal.

When the oprichniki had tortured Russia—the entire zemshchina—according to their will and pleasure so that even the Grand Prince realized it was enough, the oprichniki still had not sated themselves with the money and property of the zemskie people. If one of the zemskie people brought a suit for a thousand rubles, he would accept a hundred rubles or less, but give a receipt [to the oprichnik] for the full amount. All the petitions were set aside together with the records and receipts. [The oprichniki] had sworn to maintain no friendships with the zemskie people and to have nothing to do with them; but then the Grand Prince turned the tables and had all petitions accepted. And when the oprichniki were indebted for a thousand and had a receipt, but had not fully paid, these oprichniki had to pay the zemskie people again. The oprichniki did not at all like this situation.

34

If Moscow had not burned with everything that was in it, the zemskie people would have been able to get from the oprichniki a great deal of money and property, which the Grand Prince had ordered the oprichniki to pay because of their unjust receipts. But when Moscow burned down with all the petitions, records, and receipts, the zemskie people suffered the loss.[46]

Then the Grand Prince began to wipe out all the chief people of the oprichnina. Prince Afanasii Viazemskii died in chains in the town of Gorodets. Aleksei [Basmanov] and his son [Fedor], with whom the Grand Prince indulged in lewdness, were killed. Maliuta Skuratov was shot near Weissenstein [Paide] in Livonia. He was the pick of the bunch, and according to the Grand Prince's order, he was remembered in church. Prince Mikhail, the son of the Grand Prince's brother-in-law from the Circassian land,[47] was chopped to death by the harquebusiers with axes or halberds. Prince Vasilii Temkin was drowned. Ivan Saburov was murdered. Peter Seisse was hanged from his own court gate opposite the bedroom. Prince Andrei Ovtsyn was hanged in the Arbatskaya street of the oprichnina. A living sheep was hung next to him. The marshal Bulat wanted to marry his sister to the Grand Prince. He was killed and his sister was raped by five hundred harquebusiers. The captain of the harquebusiers, Kuraka Unkovskii, was killed and stuck under the ice. In the previous year [name unclear] was eaten by dogs at the Karinskii guard post of Aleksandrova Sloboda. Grigorii Griaznoi was killed and his son

---

[46] In the manuscript, the preceding paragraph comes later, out of context; it stands after the next two paragraphs, before "All kinds of merchants . . . . "

[47] Temriuk Cherkasskii was Ivan's father-in-law, not his brother-in-law.

Nikita was burned alive. His brother Vasilii was captured by the Crimean Tatars. The scribe and clerk Posnik Suvorov was killed at the Land Chancellery. Osip Il'in was shamefully executed in the Court Chancellery.

All the chief men of the oprichnina and zemshchina and all those who were to be killed were first publicly whipped in the marketplace until they signed over all their money and property, if they had any, to the Treasury of the Grand Prince. Those who had no money and property were killed in front of churches, in the street, or in their homes, whether asleep or awake, and were thrown into the street. The cause of the death, and whether it was legal or not, was written on a note, which was then pinned to the clothes of the corpse. The body had to lie in the street day and night as a warning to the people.

All kinds of merchants were wronged, [both Ivan's] and foreigners who continually come from other countries to trade in his land. The Grand Prince would not tolerate any other merchants alongside his own, except those who traded at Narva with the Germans, French, and English and with other foreigners from overseas.[48] And he taxed them as he saw fit—some more, some less.

Merchants from Foreign Countries

The Turkish merchant Chilibei was expelled from Moscow. He had not been paid for the goods the Grand

---

[48] In 1558, when he invaded Livonia, Ivan conquered Narva, a port on the Finnish Gulf belonging to the Livonian Order. Until 1581, when Narva was taken by the Swedes, the Russians were thus able to maintain direct commercial relations with merchants from Western Europe. The northern route to Russia around Norway was still used, but it was less suited to commerce than was Narva.

Prince had received from him. He had to leave at once in disgrace, although the people of his country had the right to buy for money all the prisoners taken by the Russians in Lithuania and Poland as well as those from Sweden, likewise those from Livonia and other surrounding lands, and to carry them off to their own and other countries.

A number of Siberian merchants were killed, and their sables were retained in the Treasury of the Grand Prince.

Englishmen came from Persia and traveled to Kholmogory.[49] When they came to the Volga River, a Russian Cossack [*Wiltfeldischer*] chief appeared with his harquebusiers and offered to guide them and protect them from the Circassian Tatars, the Nogais, and the Lugovye and Nagornye Cheremisians. The Englishmen liked this proposal very much. The chief with his harquebusiers, therefore, came aboard the English ship, which was loaded with genuine silk cloth and spices, and wounded a number of the Englishmen. He kept the skipper and steersman, and ran back [downstream] again with the ship and goods.

The Grand Prince took a lot of money and property from the English company for his Treasury. The Queen [Elizabeth of England] sent an inquiry to the Grand Prince asking why he did it. The Grand Prince answered the ambassador thus: "Opal'nye dengi ne otdadut,"— that is, "Whatever money falls into disgrace will not be returned."[50]

---

[49] The English undertook several commercial expeditions to Persia via Russia in the sixteenth century. The Englishmen to whom Staden refers were returning from Persia to Kholmogory after one of these ventures.

[50] The Russian actually reads "The confiscated money will not be returned."

The Elector Duke August [of Saxony] sent the Grand Prince a set of barber or surgical instruments via a citizen of Leipzig named Caspar König. Everything about them was artfully made and gilded. This Caspar König received nothing from the Grand Prince. The keeper of the mint at Reval, Paul Gulden, arrived with jewels and they were taken from him.

In the podkletnye sela [court estates], which belong to the household, there have always been princes and boyars. The peasants of the metropolitan and the bishops, as well as those of the monasteries, whether [they live] on votchiny or pomestia, are divided into sokhi. In the cities, where merchants or townsmen live, one hundred houses make up one sokha. In the country all farmlands, meadows, woods, and fisheries are reckoned according to whether the land is good or bad. This land is also divided into sokhi, and every sokha in the entire land has its own descriptive name.[51] From every registered sokha in the country, the Grand Prince collected the full tribute, although many hundreds of thousands lay vacant.[52] If one person, therefore, was found living in a sokha, or on the land of the metropolitan, a bishop, or monastery, whether the person was ecclesiastical or lay, he had to pay for the entire sokha; likewise the princes and boyars of the Grand Prince, although they had to give personal military service from their estates. If they did not have any peasants on their estates, they still had to pay for all the

[51] Although it is unlikely that every sokha had its own name, Staden's description of the sokhi is quite accurate.

[52] Because of the troubled times, heavy taxation, and the open frontier, much of central Russia became almost depopulated as peasants left their land and sought relief elsewhere. Those who remained were obliged to pay the taxes due from the entire sokha, and this further contributed to peasant flight.

sokhi assigned to them, even though they gave personal military service. And those who did not appear at the muster were deprived of their estates and beaten publicly in the marketplace or in the camp, with lashes and whips. Even if one was deathly ill, he had to be carried or led to the muster.

If a sokha was found empty, it was reckoned with the others in the district, where people did live. They had to pay for the empty and wasted sokhi. At present, more vacant sokhi than populated sokhi can be found in Russia. The cross-kissers—that is, the jurors who sit at the customshouses—cannot pay.[53] The sokhi in the cities and villages must pay for them in full.

There are post stations throughout the length and breadth [of the country] where volunteers live with very good horses, with which a person can go from Moscow in six days to a neighboring frontier or from the frontier to Moscow. Each iam—or post station—lies twenty to fifty versts from the next. The iamy—or post stations— cost the Grand Prince a considerable amount of money each year to maintain. The sokhi have to maintain them now. They have to boil saltpeter to make gunpowder as well. The Treasury used to provide everything necessary for that. Now the sokhi have to manage it completely.

When the Grand Prince went touring his land or to war, his podkletnye sela formerly had to supply all kinds of provision. Now his sokhi have to provide everything. Each sokha is charged with hiring one, two, or three peasants who will, without fail, always serve with the artillery by pulling the guns. And the *pososhnyi* fellow or

[53] Cross-kissers (*tseloval'niki*) were persons elected by the local population to carry certain judicial and financial responsibilities. They solemnized their promise to serve honestly by kissing the cross.

peasant who is hired by the *pososhnye*[54] people must give guarantees to those in the sokha when he receives the money [from them]. On the other hand, the people in the sokha have to guarantee the captain in charge of those who serve with the artillery that the hired men will remain with the guns and stay whether living or dead. This guarantee is drawn up for both parties by a notary and signed by witnesses.

At present the monasteries have to supply the Grand Prince with soldiers for the field according to the extent of their estates.

During the famine and plague, all the surrounding frontiers were guarded to prevent anyone from escaping from the oprichnina to another country, and whoever was seized on the Polish border was impaled. Many were hanged.

The Grand Prince lacks nothing; for as the common Russian proverb goes: "Gospodarskoe ne izgorit, na more ne utonet,"—that is, "The lord does not burn up and does not sink at sea." They likewise say: "Vedaet Bog da gospodar." That is the same as *Cor domini in manu dei*.[55]

Before the Grand Prince began the oprichnina, the city of Moscow, along with the palace and the surround-

---

[54] *Pososhnye* people were those who lived within sokhi. Those persons serving the tsar—whether princes, boyars, or common gunners and servants—were not taxed. Consequently, the nobles' manors were not part of sokhi, although the nobles' peasants were pososhnye people. The houses of the more common servitors of the tsar, who usually lived in cities or towns, were painted white to indicate their exemption from taxes.

[55] The Latin means "The heart of the ruler is in the hands of God." The Russian saying can be translated "Only God and the sovereign know." Staden's Latin was probably better than his Russian.

ing suburbs, was built thus: in the east the city had a double gate. The city was broad in the north. The palace lay in the south beyond the river. There was another double gate in the west. There were three gates in the palace, one to the west and two in the north.[56] A square and market [Red Square] extended through the entire city from the east gate to the west gate. Only one church stood before the palace in this square. It was round and built with galleries. The first gallery outside was beautifully made and contained many sacred figures, which were ornamented with gold, jewels, pearls, and silver. The procession of the metropolitan with all the bishops occurred every year at this temple. A number of persons lay buried under the gallery. Wax candles burned by these graves day and night. [The bodies] do not decay, so the Russians say, and are considered very holy. The Russians pray to them day and night. Many bells hang in this temple.

There, where the temple stands, the square rises up like a small mountain. In the same square, not far from the temple, stand a number of cannons with which one can shoot over the wall of the east gate and over the Moscow River.

The leaders of the zemshchina were executed and killed in this square. The square, from the west—or lion —gate up to the temple, was then encircled and occupied by all the harquebusiers from the oprichnina. The dead remained lying naked in the square as a warning to the people, and afterward, in the field, they were piled up in a ditch.

One of the gates to the palace was near this temple.

[56] Although Staden says there were three gates, he describes the four there actually were.

There was another church in the east as well as other Russian churches.[57] Then came the most prominent chancelleries, all built of wood except for one of stone: the Chancellery for Kazan, the Criminal Affairs Chancellery, the Military Chancellery, the Land Chancellery, the Court Treasury, the Court Chancellery, and the chancellery to which all the signed petitions from the Grand Prince came. Beyond that stood the church in which the dead grand princes lay. Beyond that was the State Treasury.

In front of this church and the State Treasury everyone who owed something to the Treasury was punished. Then there was another double church with a vaulted staircase. The vault and one side of the left wall, up to the door and the entrance to the lower church, were painted with figures of lifeless-looking saints. From there one could go through the vaulted passage to the four-sided terrace that was in front of the hall where the Grand Prince usually ate dinner. This terrace rested on vaults, was without a roof, and was paved with stone. Every morning the Grand Prince went to the church, which was covered with gilded copper. The hall of the Grand Prince was wooden. Opposite the hall, to the east, stood a mansion in ruins. Stairs led down from the south end of the terrace into the cellar, kitchens, and bakery. Another passage led from the west end of the terrace to a great hall, which was covered with copper and was always open. Here, [extending] from the passage in the middle, was a four-sided porch upon which the Grand Prince, at great feasts, usually walked back and forth in his array with many princes and boyars in *blianten*—gold brocade. The Grand Prince also had a very beautiful and

[57] Staden is now describing the buildings in the Kremlin, which he calls the palace.

exquisite staff, set with three enormous gems. Each prince
or boyar held in his hand a staff, the sign that distinguished a ruler. Now, new men, who once were servants
of the former [aristocrats, disgraced or executed by
Ivan,] walk with the Grand Prince.[58] The porch had a
folding lattice gate leading to the other churches of the
palace. Behind the porch was a gate leading through the
passage to the square where the cellars, kitchens, and
bakery were.

Further on stood another church with five towers;
four were covered with lead, and the fifth, which stood
in the middle, was gilded. Above the church door was
a gilded icon depicting Mary.

Beyond that was the palace of the metropolitan with
all its chancelleries. The gate that led to the oprichnina
court was behind this. One could ride across the small
stream Neglinna there. The bridge over this stream was
of stone. It was the only stone bridge I saw in the entire
country.

Along the inside of the west wall, up to the other gate
that leads into the city, there were several hundred grain
bins that belonged to the oprichnina court.

Here [in the Kremlin] were a number of monasteries
where the grand princes and other great lords were generally buried. A church with a round red tower stood
in the middle of the palace. All the large bells that the
Grand Prince took from Livonia hung in this tower. Near
this tower were the Livonian artillery that the Grand
Prince seized in Fellin when he captured the Master [of
the Livonian Order] Wilhelm Fürstenberg. They stood

[58] Although Ivan IV did not categorically support the petty nobility
and oppress the aristocracy (both were in the oprichnina as well as in
the zemshchina), there was a tendency for the lesser nobility to rise,
during his reign and later.

there uncovered, just for show. Also near this tower sat all the scribes who every day wrote petitions, bonds, and receipts for one and all for money. They were all under oath [i.e., they were notaries]. All the petitions in the entire country were written in the name of the Grand Prince. Near this tower or church all the common debtors were chastised or judged; and all debtors in all places were chastised until a priest sacrificed and the bells rang [for mass].

Between the tower and the church hung another bell, which was the largest in the country. When the bell was rung on great feast days, the Grand Prince in his array, and the princes and boyars, accompanied by priests carrying the holy cross and banners before them, made their way to the church in this square.

On the day of Saints Simon and Jude [October 28], the Grand Prince, the metropolitan, the bishops, the priests, the princes, and the boyars in their array customarily usher out or take leave of summer and receive winter with crosses and banners. This is the Russian New Year's Day.[59] The foreigners who have not received an estate have to demand a new allowance chit [on this day].

Then another gate led from the palace to the city. The walls of the palace and city were built around with loopholes, everything covered with burned red brick. The double gate was here, and within the moat beneath the walls stood the lions that the Queen of England sent to the Grand Prince. The elephant that came from Arabia used to stand by this gate.

The lower court house—or Zemskii Dvor—and the arsenal were beyond that. Behind this was the [word illegible]—or printing office. Then came a tower—or

[59] New Year's Day at that time in Russia was on September 1. The feast day to which Staden refers was on October 28.

fortress—full of powder. The north gate was beyond that. From here to the next—or middle—gate were the courts of many princes and boyars. Here large prisons just like courts were built, and many of those captured in the fighting in Livonia were kept in them. During the day the gatekeeper had to let them run free inside, and at night he locked them in chains. The torture chamber was also here. From here to the third gate in the north there were all kinds of houses and courts. Still another large court was built in this street. Captive inside were [Stanislav] Dovoina and a number of other Poles, together with their women, who were led to Moscow when the Grand Prince took and conquered Polotsk. The court of the English who travel to Kholmogory was beyond that; and still farther on, the Mint.

Behind all of these there were rows of trading stalls. Each row had one item of trade. Rows of trading stalls also extended along the square [Red Square], in front of the palace.

Every day in the square there were numerous youths with many horses. A person could rent one for money and hurry off to a surrounding suburb to fetch something, such as a document, letter, or receipt, and return immediately to the chancellery at the palace.

A court was recently constructed in the middle of the city in which cannon were to be founded.

Barriers were set up in all the streets so that during the evening or at night no one could ride or walk past them unless he knew the guard. If a person was arrested while drunk, he was kept in the guardhouse until morning and was then sentenced to corporal punishment.

All cities and suburbs were built in this way.

All the bishops of the country had their own special houses in this city. Each of the most prominent monas-

teries of the country also had a special house in the city
or suburbs; likewise all priests and sextons, all voevody
and military commanders, all clerks and scribes, all doormen, and also about two thousand lesser nobles who had
to be in attendance at the various chancelleries every day.
When something happened in the country, instructions
were given to these [petty nobles] and they were immediately dispatched. Likewise [there were the houses
of] all hunters, stableboys, gardeners, tapsters, and
cooks. The houses of ambassadors and those of a great
many foreigners who served the Grand Prince were
there. All these houses were free of service obligations.
When the oprichnina was established, however, all those
living on the west side of the little stream Neglinna had
to leave their houses without compensation, and flee to
the surrounding suburbs that had not been taken into the
oprichnina. This applied to lay people and ecclesiastics
alike. Those who were taken into the oprichnina, whether
they lived in the city or the suburbs, could leave the zemshchina and freely move into the houses in the oprichnina, selling their houses in the zemshchina or disman-
tling them and moving them to the oprichnina.

Then there was a great famine and plague, and many
houses and monasteries were abandoned. Many rich
merchants left their homes and fled here and there in
the country, because of the order the Grand Prince sent
to the zemshchina from the oprichnina [i.e., the order
establishing the oprichnina]. The misery was so great
that everyone in the zemshchina sought a place to flee to.

The Khan of the Crimea learned of this situation and
arrived before Moscow with the [father-in-law] of the
Grand Prince, Temriuk from the Circassian land. The
Grand Prince fled with all his soldiers from the oprich-

nina to the unfortified city of Rostov. The Tatar Khan first set fire to the Grand Prince's summer house Kolomenskoe, which lies one mile from the city.[60] Then everyone living outside [the city] in the suburbs—clerics from monasteries, laymen, oprichniki, and zemskie people—fled and ran to one place [i.e., into the city]. The next day [the Crimean Khan] had the palisades or suburbs, which were very large, set afire. Many monasteries and churches were there. The city, the palace [Kremlin], the oprichnina court, and the suburbs burned down completely in six hours. It was a great disaster, because no one could escape. Not three hundred persons capable of bearing arms remained alive. The bells in the temple and the walls they hung on [collapsed], and the stones killed those who sought refuge there. The temple and church tower, together with all the ornaments and icons, were completely burned out. Only the walls remained standing. The bells that hung in the tower in the middle of the palace melted, cracked, and fell to the ground, some in pieces. The largest fell and broke apart. The bells in the oprichnina [court] fell to the ground; likewise all the bells that hung in wooden churches and monasteries inside and outside the city. The tower—or fortress—where powder was stored exploded and the people in the cellar were asphyxiated. Outside [the walls] many Tatars, who pillaged monasteries and churches in the oprichnina and zemshchina, . . . [unfinished sentence].[61] In a word, there is not a man alive who can imagine Moscow's misery at this time.

[60] About five English miles. All miles referred to in the text are German miles. Staden is usually inaccurate in giving distances.

[61] Polosin understood this to mean that many Tatars also perished in the fire.

The Tatar Khan also had all the still-unthreshed grain on the Grand Prince's estates burned. The Tatar Kahn Devlet-Girei then returned to the Crimea taking with him much money and property and many hundreds of thousands of prisoners. He devastated the entire Ryazan land. [This all occurred in May 1571.]

The Oprichnina Court Building

At a gunshot's distance west of the palace, in a square on high ground, the Grand Prince ordered the houses of many princes, boyars, and merchants destroyed. The square was walled; the first six feet from the ground were of hewn stone; the next twelve feet of burned brick. Above, the walls were brought together to a point without a roof or loopholes and they were 780 feet long and broad. There were three gates, one in the east, the second in the south, and the third in the north. The north gate stood opposite the palace, and was fastened with tin-covered iron plates. Inside, where the gate was opened and closed, two enormous oak logs were set in the ground, and two large holes [were cut] through them. A bar, which was set into the wall, could be pulled or put through the large logs to the other side on the right, when the gates were closed. These gates were covered with lead. On these gates, there were two carved and painted lions, the eyes of which were set with mirrors. There was also a double-headed eagle, carved from wood and painted black, with outspread wings. One [lion] stood with its mouth open, looking toward the zemshchina. The other looked in the same way toward the [oprichnina] court. Between these two lions the black, double [-headed] eagle stood with its breast toward the zemshchina, wings extended.[62]

Within this structure three vast buildings were constructed. On the peak of each stood a double [-headed] eagle, carved from wood and painted black, with its breast facing the zemshchina. From these main buildings a passage led over the court to the southeast corner. There, in front of the room and hall, a small cottage with a porch was built even with the ground. For the length of this cottage and porch the wall was three feet lower to catch the sun and a breeze. The Grand Prince usually ate here in the morning and at noon. In front of this cottage was a cellar full of large pieces of wax. This was the Grand Prince's special square. Because of the dampness, this square was covered with white sand two feet deep.

The south gate was only large enough for a man to ride in and out. All the chancelleries were built here, and all debtors were chastised [here] with sticks or cudgels until a priest began to say mass and a bell pealed. In addition, petitions of the oprichniki were signed here and sent to the zemshchina. What was signed here was just, and, in accordance with the mandate, was not questioned in the zemshchina.[63]

Here and outside, the servants of the princes and boyars kept all their horses. When the Grand Prince rode

---

[62] Staden's description of the oprichnina court is unique. Because the court existed for such a short period of time (from 1566 or 1567 to 1571) it is perhaps not especially unusual that other contemporaries failed to describe it.

[63] The administration of the zemshchina was parallel, although not entirely parallel, to the oprichnina administration.

to the zemshchina, they could immediately follow him [on horseback]. The princes and boyars were not permitted to enter or leave the [oprichnina] court by the east gate. That was exclusively for the horses and sleigh of the Grand Prince.

The structure extended this far to the south. Then came a small gate that was nailed shut on the inside. There was no gate on the west side, but there was a large square without buildings.

On the north side there was a large gate fastened with tin-covered iron plates. Here were all the kitchens, cellars, bakeries, and baths. In the cellars there were various kinds of mead and several [areas] full of ice. Upstairs there were large chambers built of planks with stone supports, and all the planks were cut through with carvings of foliage. All the animals and fish were hung here; from the Caspian Sea come most of the fish, such as beluga [white sturgeon], sturgeon, sevruga [stellated sturgeon], and sterlet [small sturgeon]. There was a small door here through which food and drink could be carried from the kitchens, cellars, and bakeries to the court on the right. The bread that [Ivan] himself eats is unsalted.

There were two staircases here, which led up to the large chambers. One was opposite the east gate. A small scaffold like a square table stood in front of this stairway. The Grand Prince climbed on this to mount and dismount his horse. These stairways were flanked by two columns upon which the roof and a wooden vault rested; and on the columns and the vault there were carvings of foliage. All the [upper] rooms opened out on a balcony that extended to the wall. The Grand Prince could go from the rooms onto this balcony and over the wall to the church, which stood outside the walls in front of the court in the east. This church was cross-shaped, and its foundation was eight logs deep. It stood unroofed for three years. The bells that the Grand Prince robbed and took from Great Novgorod hung near this church. The other staircase was on the right as one came through the east gate. Every night at the foot of these staircases, below the balcony, five hundred harquebusiers guarded the chamber or hall where the Grand Prince usually ate. The princes and boyars had the night watch on the south side.

This entire structure was built of pure fir. All this wood was cut from a forest called Klin. Near this forest, eighteen miles from Moscow on the main road to Tver and Great Novgorod, there is an unfortified settlement also called Klin, and a post station. The only tools used by the carpenters or construction workers for this beautiful building were an axe, chisels, a plane, and a piece of iron like a crooked knife set in a handle.

When the Tatar Khan Devlet-Girei had the suburbs and the monasteries outside set afire, as soon as a monastery caught fire a bell would peal three times, again and again, until the fire reached this mighty court and church. The fire spread from here [the oprichnina court] to the entire city of Moscow and the palace [Kremlin]. All ringing of bells was forgotten. All the bells in this church melted into the ground. No one could escape this fire. The lions that had been within the moat beneath the walls were found dead in the marketplace. After the conflagration, not a single cat or dog remained in any area within the walls.

Thus, the wishes of the zemskie people and the threat of the Grand Prince were fulfilled. The zemskie people had wished that this [oprichnina] court would burn down. The Grand Prince had threatened to give the zemskie people a fire that they would not be able to extinguish. The Grand Prince thought that he wanted to continue to treat the zemshchina as he had at first, that he wanted to root out all the injustice of the rulers and commanders of the country. He therefore did not want their families, who had not justly and truly served his forefathers, to remain in the country any longer. He wanted to ensure that the new rulers would judge the law as he established it—according to the law books, without donations, gifts, or bribes. The rulers of the zemshchina meant to oppose and obstruct, and they hoped that the [oprichnina] court would burn down, that there would be an end to the power of the oprichnina, and that the Grand Prince would rule according to their wishes and pleasure. Almighty God then sent the instrument, the Crimean Khan Devlet-Girei, through whom this was brought about.

With that the oprichnina came to an end,[64] and no one was permitted to allude to it with a single word under pain of the following punishment: he was stripped to the waist and driven through the marketplace with whips. All the oprichniki had to return the votchiny of the zemskie people; and all the zemskie people who were still alive got back their votchiny, which had been devastated and plundered by the oprichniki.

[64] In this passage Staden says that the oprichnina was abolished after the burning of Moscow in 1571. Later he states that it was abolished after the campaign on the Oka River in 1572, which is the correct year. Since this discrepancy could hardly be attributed to a lapse of memory—the event was too important to Staden's personal interests—it must be an error in copying, and the passage should probably stand elsewhere, perhaps on p. 55, just before the mention of the deaths of Vorotynskii and Odoevskii.

The city of Moscow was burned out [on May 24, 1571], and a year later the Crimean Khan returned to conquer Russia. This time he was met by the soldiers of the Grand Prince on the Oka River, seventy versts or a Russian day's ride from the city of Moscow. For more than fifty miles along this Oka River the banks were fortified so: two four-foot palisades were set up with a two-foot space between them. The earth dug from behind the rear palisade was thrown between the two and the space was thus filled. The palisades were constructed by the princes and boyars according to the extent of their estates. The harquebusiers therefore could lie behind the two palisades or entrenchments and shoot the Tatars as they swam across the river.

The Russians intended to resist the Crimean Khan at this river and entrenchment, but they failed. The Crimean Khan drew up opposite us on the other side of the Oka. The Khan's chief commander, Divei-Murza, with a large force, crossed the river far from us so that the entrenchments were useless. They came on us from behind, through Serpukhov. Then the fun began and it lasted fourteen days and nights. One voevoda after another had to struggle constantly with the Khan's troops. If the Russians had not had the barricade of wagons, the Crimean Khan would have killed us [or] taken us bound as prisoners into the Crimea and all of Russia would have been his.

We captured the Crimean Khan's chief commanders, Divei-Murza and Chaz Bulat, but no one knew their language. [We thought Divei-Murza] was a lesser noble. The next day a Tatar who was the servant of Divei-Murza was captured. "How long will the Khan hold out?" he was asked. "Why ask me about that?" the Tatar

answered. "Ask my lord, Divei-Murza, whom you captured yesterday." Then everyone was ordered to bring
his prisoners forward. The Tatar pointed at Divei-Murza
and said, "He is Divei-Murza." Then Divei-Murza was
asked, "Are you Divei-Murza?" "No," he answered, "I
am a modest nobleman." Divei-Murza thereupon became impudent and cheeky. He said to Prince Mikhail
Vorotynskii and all the military commanders, "You
peasants, how can you be so insolent and fight against
your lord, the Crimean Khan?" "You are a prisoner,"
they answered, "and you still threaten?" Divei-Murza
answered and said, "If the Crimean Khan were captured
instead of me, I would want to free him and lead [you]
peasants as captives to the Crimea." "How could you do
that?" the military commanders asked him. "I would
starve you out of the wagon fortress in five or six days,"
Divei-Murza answered. He had certainly seen that the
Russians had eaten their horses when they should have
ridden them against the enemy. The Russians then became despondent.

The districts and cities of Russia had already all been
divided among the nobles who were with the Crimean
Khan, and each was assigned what he should receive. A
number of Turkish gentlemen who wanted to observe
this were with the Crimean Khan. They were sent by the
Turkish Sultan at the request of the Crimean Khan. The
Crimean Khan had boasted to the Turkish Sultan that
he would conquer all of Russia and lead the Grand
Prince to the Crimea as a prisoner and occupy Russia
with his nobles.

The Nogai Tatars who were with the Khan were dis-
pleased, because the booty had not been divided equally
when they helped the Khan burn Moscow in the previous
year.

The Grand Prince fled again—just as he did when Moscow was burned—to Great Novgorod, one hundred miles from Moscow, and again left his troops and country to their fate. From Great Novgorod the Grand Prince sent our field commander, Prince Mikhail Vorotynskii, an untruthful message: [Vorotynskii] should hold out and [Ivan] would send King Magnus with 40,000 horsemen to help. The Crimean Khan intercepted this message and became frightened and despondent, and because of it he returned to the Crimea.

Every corpse that had a cross around its neck was buried at the monastery that lies near Serpukhov. The others were eaten by birds. Every Russian prince and boyar who had been shot, hacked, or wounded by the enemy in the front of his body had his estates increased or improved; but those who were wounded from behind had their estates reduced, and remained in disgrace for a long time. Those who were so wounded or shot that they were lame or crippled became officials in the cities and districts and were replaced on the military muster roll by the healthy officials of the cities and districts. All the sons of the princes or boyars who were twelve years old were also given estates and were entered on the military muster roll; and if they failed to appear at muster in person, they were punished just like their fathers. No one in the entire country, not even one who had received nothing from the Grand Prince, was free from service.

Then the two field commanders, Prince Mikhail Vorotynskii and Nikita Odoevskii, were killed.

Although the Almighty God has punished Russia so severely and heavily that it is beyond description, still the present Grand Prince has managed so that in all of Russia, or in his government, there is one faith, one weight, and one measure, that he alone rules, that everything he orders is done and everything he prohibits is not done. No one, neither cleric nor layman, stands against him. How long such a government can continue, only the Almighty God knows.

How the Grand Prince Took and Conquered
Kazan and Astrakhan

The Grand Prince had a city built with wooden walls, citadels, gates—everything just like an actual city—and had all the wooden beams marked from top to bottom. He then took the city apart, put it on rafts, and let it float down the Volga together with troops and large cannon [1551]. When he came before Kazan, he had this city put together, and filled everything [i.e., the fortifications] with earth. He garrisoned this city with Russians and cannons, and then returned to Moscow. He called the city Sviyazhsk. Since the people of Kazan lost their freedom of movement, they continually joined battle and fought the Russians.

The Grand Prince then set out in force and came once more before the city of Kazan. He undermined the city and blew it up. He thus conquered the city and took the Khan Shig-Alei prisoner, giving the city to the soldiers as a prize [1552].[65] The city was plundered and its inhabitants were murdered, stripped naked, and placed in a heap. Then the ankles or feet of the corpses were tied together, and afterward a long log was taken and stuck between their legs. They were then thrown into the Volga, twenty, thirty, forty, or fifty on a log. The logs with

[65] The Khan then was actually Edigei, the last khan of Kazan. Shig-Alei was his predecessor. After Ivan IV conquered Kazan, Shig-Alei was given Kasimov—not Zvenigorod as Staden states. Early in the Livonian war, Shig-Alei was the commander of Ivan's Tatar cavalry.

the bodies floated downstream. The bodies hung from the logs in the water, only the feet showing above, where they were bound.

The Khan of Astrakhan [Derbysh-Alei] learned of this. Seeing that the people of Astrakhan might end up keeping their feet dry in this way, he became terrified and fled to the Khan of the Crimea, leaving Astrakhan undefended. The Russians came and garrisoned Astrakhan with troops and cannon [1556].

The Grand Prince returned again to Moscow, leaving much gold brocade, silver, gold, and all kinds of silk cloth with his commanders in Kazan and Astrakhan.

Although these two khanates were taken, a great many *mirzi*—that is, kniazi or Tatar princes—still lived in them, and [the countryside] was still in their possession. They could not be subdued easily, because the land extended as far and wide as the Lugovye and Nagornye Cheremisians. The Russian commanders in the cities of Kazan and Astrakhan became friendly with a number of Tatars, invited them as guests, and gave them brocades and silver bowls, as though they were nobles or men of high rank. They were permitted to return to their lands in order to show the presents to others, who did not consider themselves subjects [of the Grand Prince], much less his servants. When the others saw that the voevody and commanders of the Grand Prince had given presents and shown such honor to their people, who were of lower rank than themselves, they thought they would [get more?] [Sentence incomplete.] The commanders in Kazan and Astrakhan became aware of this and invited all the prominent mirzi—or kniazi—that is, princes and gentlemen—to come and receive the favor and presents of the Grand Prince.

The most prominent nobles went to Kazan and were

well received. They thought it would go with them as [it had] with the others. As soon as they got the presents, they wanted to return home; but when they were good and drunk, having drunk altogether too much brandy and mead, which they were not accustomed to as the Russians are, a few hundred harquebusiers came in and shot all these Tatar guests, who were the most prominent chiefs.

With this the Grand Prince brought the two khanates to obedience until the Crimean Khan came and burned the Grand Prince's city of Moscow. Then the [Tatar] people rose up and advanced out of the two khanates into the land of the Grand Prince, burning many unfortified settlements and carrying off thousands of Russians as captives, in addition to killing many. The opinion is that they [the people of Kazan and Astrakhan] shall succeed [in freeing themselves], because the Crimean Khan burned down Moscow.

The following year [1572] the Khan again came out of the Crimea to conquer Russia. To all his merchants and to many others he gave instructions to travel with their goods to Kazan and Astrakhan and trade without paying duty; for he was Khan and the lord of all Russia. When the Tatar Khan failed, however, all these merchants in Kazan and Astrakhan were plundered. There were many and various goods found with [the merchants] that were unfamiliar even to the Russians; and many did not recognize the goods.

Although the troops of his royal majesty of Sweden [John III, 1568–92] were camped outside Wesenberg [in Livonia], the Grand Prince nevertheless advanced with his entire army to this frontier and sent into these two countries [Kazan and Astrakhan] to ask what they intended to do. Did they intend to obey him or not? If they wanted to be obedient, they should then hand over all the chief leaders who started the affair. If not, he would advance with his army and kill everyone. They must also set all Russians free.

Then many chiefs who had not been involved in the affair came and promised on behalf of the country to arrest all their chiefs, and the Grand Prince should send and have all the Russian prisoners taken back. The Grand Prince had all the Russian prisoners sent back to Russia, and had all the Tatar soldiers killed. He had the principal leaders pulled apart with a catapult and had many others impaled. This was a warning to the country.

The country of the Grand Prince is so situated in these lands that he cannot injure the Turks in his lands and he also cannot reach [the Turks' lands]. The Nogais lie in the east. The land of the Circassian people lies in the southeast. Further east and to the south lies Shemakha; and beyond the [Caspian] Sea [are] Bukhara and the [lands of the Persian] Kizilbashes.[66] The Crimea lies in the south. Also in the south lie Lithuania and the city of Kiev; in the west, Poland; in the north, Sweden, Norway, the coast of the White Sea [which I have] described, and the Solovetskii monastery. In the northeast lie Mangazeya, Takhcheya, and the Samoyeds.[67]

The Nogais are a free people without an emperor, king, or lords. Previously they served the Grand Prince

[66] The Kizilbashes are members of a Shiitic sect. Their name, "Kizilbashes" (in Turkish, "redheads"), probably came from their red caps. They lived in Persia in Staden's time, and many still live in Afghanistan and Turkey.

[67] Mangazeya, a town near modern Khalmer Sede, was named for a local Samoyed tribe. "Takhcheya" refers to northwestern Siberia, beyond the Ob.

by freely raiding Lithuania, Poland, Livonia, and the frontiers of the Swedish empire. When the Crimean Khan burned Moscow, there were 30,000 Nogai horsemen with him. They also used to bring herds of many thousands of horses to Russia for sale. The Grand Prince took every tenth horse as a tariff, and if he wanted more horses than this, his jurors paid for them from the Treasury.

The Grand Prince had [as his wife] the daughter of Prince Mikhail Temriukovich from the Circassian country.[68] [The latter] was also with the Crimean Khan when he burned Moscow.

The Persian Kizilbashes, the Bukharans, and the Shemakhans—these people have always traded in Russia. Most of their wares are gold brocades, various kinds of silk cloth, spices, and much more. The Grand Prince takes the tenth part of all goods as tariff.

The Grand Prince has to keep his troops on the Oka every year to resist this [Crimean] Khan. His troops previously used to meet this Khan at the Don and the Donets [Rivers] in the wild steppe between the Crimea and the Ryazan land.

If the Grand Prince should pass through Lithuania near the city of Kiev, he still would be unable to harm the Turks.

It is the Grand Prince's intention to deal with Germany as he did with Kazan, Astrakhan, Livonia, and the city of Polotsk in Lithuania. The Grand Prince arrived outside Polotsk with a strong force and large cannons. Priests with crosses, icons, and banners came from the city to the camp of the Grand Prince and surrendered

---

[68] Staden again confuses Mikhail with his father, Temriuk. Here he means Temriuk.

the city to the Grand Prince against the will of its commander, Dovoina [1563]. The Grand Prince had all the knights and soldiers taken from the city, separated from one another, and killed. They were then thrown into the [Western] Dvina. The same happened to the Jews who were there, although they offered many thousands of florins for their lives. In Lithuania the Jews kept all the taverns and customshouses. The poor people froze or died of hunger. The townsmen were led away with their wives and children to a number of cities in Russia. The commander, Dovoina, was taken to prison in Moscow. A few years later he was exchanged for a Russian prince. He had his wife disinterred from the German graveyard outside Moscow, and returned with her [body] to Poland. The townsmen and many nobles, together with their wives and children, lived for many years in prisons in irons welded with lead; and when the Grand Prince and his oprichnina troops took a number of cities, all these [people], including women and children, were killed. Their legs were cut off, because of the ice, and they were thrown into the water.

The Grand Prince would like to, and is of the opinion that he ought to, maintain friendship with the Roman Emperor until he acquires all kinds of craftsmen and so many thousands of soldiers that he can resist the Crimean Khan. He also thinks he might persuade the Roman Emperor to go to war with Poland. He would like very much to have such an advantage.

While the King of Poland was camped outside Danzig, [the Grand Prince] took the rest of Livonia.[69] Who-

[69] Ivan did not conquer all of Livonia. Shortly after this campaign he began to suffer reverses in Livonia, and he never recovered. By 1583 he had lost the entire country and had made peace with the Poles and the Swedes.

ever does not know what he then did to Livonia can simply ask.

If the Roman Empire would attack Poland, then the Grand Prince would take the city of Vilna in Lithuania and then extend [his] frontiers to Germany.

The Samoyeds have no master. These are a wild people and live on fish, birds, and reindeer. These same people shoot and catch sables in their land and bring them to sell to the Russians. They trade them for cloth, kettles, bacon, butter, helmets, and oat flour. They meet in Pustozersk, which lies in a wild place. Every year the Grand Prince receives numerous sables from this country in tribute. The country lies seven hundred miles from the city of Moscow. The man who presently collects the tribute from this country is named Petr Visloukhii. He cannot take any more from these people than they care to give. Mangazeya also has no lord. Its people also catch sables and other animals. Takhcheya is completely barren. There is not a person in the entire country. It is said that in Roman times when a person went into exile, he was sent to this land.

His royal majesty John III of Sweden sent Scottish, Swedish, and German troops, mounted and on foot, with cannon, powder, and shot, to the castle of Wesenberg in Livonia, which they were to take and conquer. As the castle was being stormed, the Scots and Germans had a falling out and began beating and killing each other, so that a few hundred remained dead on the field. This affair pleased the Russians in the castle very much and served them well. They said: "Sobaka sobaku i s'ela"—that is, "One dog has eaten the other." The troops of his royal majesty therefore had to withdraw in shame and [the affair] remained unfinished.

If the people of the Grand Prince surrender a city, a fortress, or a castle, and they return to Russia alive, they are all killed along with all their relatives and those who guaranteed the harquebusiers. They know very well that if they go over to the enemy, no one will think much of them; they know that they are going against their oath, and that in the churches of Russia on every feast day prayers will be said urging their eternal damnation.

The Grand Prince rewarded all his [men] at Wesenberg castle, especially the commander and the German interpreter, Simon Kerklin, who received from the Grand Prince two of the best German horses, four hundred den'gi, and four hundred chetverts of land.[70] He also received the right to choose the best house in Narva in Livonia. For his faithful service the Grand Prince gave the military commander the income of the entire district of Kargopol [about 500 miles north of Moscow] for a period of three years.

When the people of Kargopol heard this news, they got together a sum of money and bought two of the very best houses, which stood close together, and they arranged that one could go from one house to the other from the inside. They did that because the house that the [previous] commander had lived in for a number of years was rotten and tumbledown. In all the cities and unfortified settlements throughout the country, a nobleman customarily serves as commander, and sits and judges for a period of two or three years. During the Livonian war the Grand Prince abolished this system

---

[70] A chetvert of land is the amount that can be sown with one chetvert (about eight bushels) of seed grain. It usually was about one and one-third acres, but this varied with the quality of the land.

and commissioned jurors; for he could not spare the nobles from the war.

When the commander arrived in Kargopol, he was taken to the two purchased houses. One was for his princess and the other was for him and his servants. The commander then began to chastise the people of Kargopol, to put them to the test; and he beat them daily with cudgels, because they had permitted the commander's house to become dilapidated. The people of Kargopol secretly sent to Moscow and complained to the authorities, but nothing came of it. The commander became aware of this and he had all the priests in the district instructed not to perform a marriage without payment of twenty altin—that is, sixty mariagroschen. He instructed all the *sotskie*—that is, the chief men in the sokhi—that they should take one Russian mark for every barrel from those who wanted to brew beer. The people of Kargopol and all the nearby sokhi sent some judicious people to Moscow to complain about this to the Grand Prince personally; but again nothing came of it. The commander learned of this, and set watches on all the roads and crossroads so that those who came from the coast [of the White Sea] with salt and salmon for Moscow could not pass, and likewise those merchants taking other goods from Moscow to the coast could not pass. He thus took what he wanted of the goods. He even proposed to plunder all the merchants and peasants on the seacoast, but with this all the sokhi combined to meet force with force.

Therefore, in the district of Kargopol not much beer was brewed for three years, although everyone in the entire country enjoyed the right to have beer in the house on St. Nicholas's Day [December 6]. In cities and villages throughout the country, taverns were forbidden. Good friends, however, formed clubs and brewed beer, and assembled with their wives on holidays. Such [a club] is called a *bratchina*—that is, a brotherhood.

There was no joy at weddings. From the seacoast no salmon or salt was sent over the English route, and no goods were shipped from Moscow to the coast.[71] The commander accumulated a lot of money and property by force in three years, but had he been on good terms with the merchants and peasants he would have collected ten times more money and property; for Kargopol is a large district and most of its inhabitants are merchants. The others are peasants.

The district of Kargopol extends to the district of Vologda in the east, to the Belozersk district in the south, to Karelia in the west, and in the north up the entire length of the Onega River to the White Sea, 56 German miles away.

Whenever anyone but a Jew comes to the Russian border, he is immediately asked what he wants. If he answers that he wishes to serve the Grand Prince, he is again asked all sorts of questions. His report and speech are taken down in secret and sealed. Then he is immediately sent by post horse to Moscow, accompanied by a nobleman; this takes six or seven days. In Moscow he is secretly and extensively questioned about everything, and if his answers agree with what he said at the border, he is so much more believed and favored. His person is not considered, nor his clothes or nobility. Only what he says is given close attention. He is immediately given money for provisions—from the day he arrives at the border until he reaches Moscow. In Moscow he is given a *kormovaia pamiat'*—that is, a chit for expenses—on the day of his arrival.

[71] "The English route" is the route used by English merchants to travel inland from the coast of the White Sea.

There is a special court set up in Moscow where boiled and unboiled mead is brewed. All the foreigners receive their daily expense allowance here, according to the chits, some getting less, some more.

At the Land Chancellery, this same foreigner will get another note, which says that the Grand Prince has favored him with an estate of one hundred, two hundred, three hundred, or four hundred chetverts. He may then look around in the country or inquire where a nobleman died without heirs or was killed in battle. The wife will be given something for her maintenance, and [the estate of the deceased] will be assigned to the foreigner according to [the Grand Prince's] instructions. He plows up the winter seed in the harvest and he is given money to buy summer seed. At first he is also given a sum of money as well as clothes—broadcloth, silk cloth, some gold brocades, and caftans lined with grey fur or sable. After the harvest, the expense money is deducted.

Before Moscow was burned, the Grand Prince used to give a foreigner a house in that city. At present he is given [a plot] 102 feet long and deep in Bolvanovka where the German horsemen live—men on foot do not count. The plot is fenced in for him. Then the foreigner can build as he sees fit. If he petitions the Grand Prince, saying that he wants to build a house, he will be given something. In the house he may keep a tavern. This is forbidden to [Ivan's] people and among them it is a great disgrace.

In addition he still has his yearly allowance, and he and his servants are exempt from tariffs throughout the country.

Before this time [i.e., before the burning of Moscow] the Grand Prince also used to give many foreigners letters that exempted them from appearing in court when Russians brought charges against them, except on two days of the year—Christmas and the Feast of Saints Peter and Paul [June 29]. On these two holy days regular rules did not apply. The letter designated a special *pristav* [official of a law court] to bring the foreigner before the law, and if a pristav other than the one mentioned in the letter wanted to call the foreigner before the law, the foreigner had the right to beat the pristav in his house, to thrash him as he saw fit. If he then brought charges against the foreigner, he was again beaten or punished. A foreigner had the right to bring charges against a Russian every day. The Grand Prince thus can learn of the affairs of all his neighbors. [That is, by giving foreigners special consideration.]

On St. George's Day before Christmas, the peasants have the right to leave [November 26]. They live under the Grand Prince, the metropolitan, or whomever they choose. If that were not the case, no peasant could keep a penny in his pocket, and neither horse nor cow would be secure in its stall. A number of peasants in the country have a lot of money, but they do not brag about it at all. A peasant wants to be protected so that nothing unjust happens to him.

All peasant villages are divided into sokhi. It often occurs that three, four, five, or six peasants are part of another sokha: for one peasant lives here, another there, yet they are still registered in one sokha. A sokha contains about a thousand morgens of land inclusive of woods, meadow, and water.[72]

---

[72] One morgen equals about two acres by one reckoning, and two-thirds of an acre by another. It is uncertain which Staden means.

An example. A letter comes by post from Moscow to
the commander of a district where foreigners have estates. The commander is to inspect the sokhi, because the
Grand Prince intends to make a tour. It does not say
where. Even some of those who ride with him do not
know where he plans to go until he arrives. The sokhi
are to have a holiday on a fixed day. One sokha must
give:

1½ oxen at ½ ruble each—one ruble equals 3 reichs-
    talers;
5 sheep at [word omitted] altin each—one altin
    equals 3 mariagroschen;
2 wild geese at 10 mariagroschen each;
4 pair of pigeons at 1 mariagroschen a pair;
1 pair of ducks at 6 mariagroschen [a pair];
20 markpounds of butter at 1 mariagroschen a
    pound;
3 measures of cream at ½ mariagroschen a measure;
200 eggs at 3 mariagroschen a hundred;
4 measures of milk at ½ mariagroschen a measure;
30 pounds of bacon at ½ mariagroschen a pound;
10 Livonian pounds of honey at 30 mariagroschen
    [a pound];
12 cheeses at ½ mariagroschen each;
12 hens at 3 mariagroschen a pair;
5 markpounds of hops at 1½ mariagroschen a
    pound;
20 measures of strawberries at ½ mariagroschen
    [a measure];
7 measures of cherries for coloring mead at 5
    mariagroschen a measure;
6 cartloads of hay at 6 mariagroschen a load;
7 barrels of oats at 10 mariagroschen a barrel.

Now let a foreigner have fifty morgens of land in this sokha, and calculate what a peasant who farms ten morgens owes, in order that the other peasants are not treated unjustly.[73] Some sokhi are divided into parts. They have it better. The administrators of the estates or the bailiffs of the Russian boyars always see to it that the peasants of the foreigners carry the burden. Therefore, the foreigners' estates become depopulated on St. George's Day.

In Russia plum stones are used for reckoning. Likewise, those who keep the iamy—or post stations—must also boil saltpeter to make gunpowder, etc.[74]

When the estate of a foreigner became depopulated, the Grand Prince used to give [him] other estates where peasants lived [up to] three times. At present a foreigner can get an estate that has peasants only with great difficulty, because the land is for the most part depopulated.

Most of the foreigners in Moscow are Germans, Tatars, Circassians, and Lithuanians. Those who were of the Russian faith and were friends of the Grand Prince have been killed. The Grand Prince uses the baptized against the unbaptized, and the unbaptized against the baptized landowners and people. A foreigner is free to hold any faith he chooses, so long as he does not force his servants and maids to eat meat on the fast days, likewise on Wednesdays and Fridays.

A foreigner cannot be put to death just because he has sinned greatly. If, however, he is caught trying to flee the country, then only God can help him. His talents no longer count, and his money and property help him not at all. It seldom happens that a foreigner manages to flee the country, since the road into the country is broad and clear, but the way out is extremely narrow, even if

[73] There is, of course, no basis for such a calculation.
[74] A curious intrusion of an irrelevant sentence.

one has studied Muscovy in the greatest schools [before going there], and that is of course impossible. A person could be as learned and capable as he might wish, and he would discover this [to be true] when he reached Moscow.

Doctor Eliseus Bomelius came to the Grand Prince from England during the great plague. He had acquired a lot of money and property, and had lined his pockets well. He requested a pass from the Grand Prince, saying that he wanted to send his servant to Riga to get some medicinal herbs which he could not find in the Treasury. He took the pass himself and set out in the guise of his servant. He had changed all his money and property into gold and had it sewn into his clothes. When he arrived at the post station in Pskov, he wanted to buy some fish in the market. Although his beard was cut off [*abgeschnitten war*], he was recognized by the way he spoke. The Russians found his money, and the good doctor was led back to Moscow in chains welded with lead.

When a [foreign] merchant arrives at the border, his wares are inspected by the commander and a clerk. If they think the Grand Prince will buy them, they forward [some of] them to him by stage, and write that a merchant has arrived from this or that country with these and similar goods and he offers them at such and such a price. If they are wares that the Grand Prince wants, the merchant and his goods are dispatched by stage to Moscow along with a pristav, who sees that the goods are not taken from him; but actually he goes with him to see that he does not poke into every corner and examine every town and city along the way.

If an ambassador arrives at the border, many people are sent to meet him. They lead him, along only those roads where peasants are living, to the place where the Grand Prince will give him an audience, so that he does not learn the right route and see how desolate the country is. The ambassador is guarded this closely, and likewise his servants, so that no foreigner can reach him. Often two or three ambassadors arrive at the place where the Grand Prince will hear them. They are guarded so carefully that one ambassador does not know of the other. Even if the Grand Prince has not received the first ambassador, he still knows how he will answer the second, third, and fourth. The Grand Prince, therefore, can learn of the affairs of all the neighboring governments, but they can know nothing certain about his country.

Toropets is a city built completely of wood. Here in a swamp and a stagnant [*stehenden*] lake is the source of the large Russian River Volga and the [Western] Dvina.[75] From Toropets the Volga flows to the city of Rzheva Volodimirova [Rzhev], then to the city of Zubtsov,[76] and further to the city of Staritsa. In this district [the Grand Prince] gave votchiny and pomestia to me, Heinrich von Staden, to Andrei Kholopov, and to the princes Rudok and Menshik Obolenskii. Prince Vladimir Andreevich, whose daughter was married to Duke Magnus, lived here. Then [the Volga flows] to Tver, [Kalinin] and further to Kashin and to Kimry. Here the Grand Prince wanted to build as at Aleksandrova Sloboda. Then to Uglich and further to Mologa where

[75] The Western Dvina and the Volga do not have their sources in the same lake.
[76] The manuscript reads "Torsoch." According to Epstein, if Staden was thinking of Torzhok, he erred. I have followed Polosin, who suggests Zubtsov.

there used to be a large annual fair. Further on lies Rybnaya Sloboda, and then Romanov.[77] This unfortified settlement was given to the Tatars. Yaroslavl lies further on and then the city of Kostroma. In this district there is a small unfortified city called Lyubim, with a wooden castle. The Grand Prince gave this to the Bishop of Dorpat and the Master Wilhelm Fürstenberg for their maintenance. Then comes Nizhny Novgorod and the unfortified settlement Balakhna. Salt is boiled here. Further on lies the wooden city of Sviyazhsk; then Kazan and Astrakhan. Here the Volga empties into the Caspian through 72 mouths.

The [Western] Dvina flows from Toropets to the city of Polotsk and to the city of Vitebsk.[78] This city is presently being harried by the Grand Prince. Below this city lie the Livonian fortresses and castles that the Grand Prince has recently taken—Kreuzburg, Dünaburg, and Kokenhusen. Kirchholm is torn down. Further on lies the city of Riga. Two miles further down lies Dünamünde.[79] As soon as the Grand Prince wins this castle, the people of Riga will not be able to use the sea, and will be landlocked. Along the same route on the river [Aa—now the Gauya] in Livonia, the Grand Prince has the following cities and fortresses: Wolmar, Wenden, Treiden, Segewold, and Kremon.[80] The Grand Prince,

[77] Rybnaya Sloboda was later called Rybinsk, is now Shcherbakov. Romanov has been called Tutayev since the early 1920's.

[78] The river actually flows from Vitebsk to Polotsk.

[79] Kreuzburg is the German name for Krustpils; Dünaburg, for Daugavpils; Kokenhusen, for Koknese; and Dünamünde, for Daugavgriva.

[80] Wolmar is the German name for Valmiera; Wenden, for Cesis (Tsesis); Segewold, for Sigulda. Treiden and Kremon (whose modern names are not known) were also on the Gauya, very close together, 18–25 miles from the Baltic.

therefore, can carry heavy cannon along the river Aa up
to Riga.

The Passage or Way of the Crimean Khan Devlet-Girei to Moscow

He must first pass through the wild steppe, coming
to the Great Don [Dnieper] at Konskie Vodi [the Kon-
skaya River] and then to the Small Don [Donets] in
the Ryazan land, and further to the fortress of Tula.
Here he has three roads to Russia. If he goes to the left
he comes to Belev. If he takes the middle way, he comes
to Kaluga and Aleksin, and if he goes to the right, he
comes to the Oka River and the city of Serpukhov, which
lies a day's ride from Moscow. The troops of the Grand
Prince meet the Crimean Khan here every year. Everything is devastated by the Tatars up to this point. It is
still fourteen miles to the city of Moscow.

The Way from Poland or Lithuania to Moscow

From Smolensk to Dorogobuzh, from Dorogobuzh
to Vyazma, from Vyazma to Rzheva Volodimirova
[Rzhev]. So far, up to the small river Boina, [the land]
belongs to the crown of Poland. From Rzhev to Zvenigorod. This unfortified city was given to the Khan of
Kazan, Shig-Alei, for his maintenance after the conquest
of Kazan and Astrakhan.[81] From there it is still eight
miles to the city of Moscow.

Another [Way]

From Porkhov to Toropets, further to Velikiye Luki,

[81] It was actually given to Derbysh-Alei, former Khan of Astrakhan.

then to Staritsa; from there to Volokolamsk or to the Osipov monastery; then to the post station Ilinskii, which is ten miles from Moscow.

[*The Way from*] *Sweden*

One goes from Noteborg [now Petrokrepost], Vyborg, or Karelia to the Tikhvinskii-Uspenskii monastery.[82] The monastery lies far [from the road] on the right side. One then comes to the main road that goes from Great Novgorod to Moscow.

[82] "Precista Tiffnia" in the manuscript

III. [*A Plan for the Conquest of Russia*]

A plan to prevent the Crimean Khan from conquering Russia with the help and assistance of the Turkish Sultan, the Nogais, and Prince Mikhail [actually Temriuk] Cherkasskii, to prevent him from carrying off the Grand Prince and his two sons [Ivan and Fedor] to the Crimea as prisoners, and to prevent him from seizing the large treasury.

Most eminent, mighty, and unconquerable Roman Emperor, King of Bohemia and Hungary, our most noble lord, etc. Your Imperial Roman Majesty sees from this account of mine how violently and cruelly the Crimean Khan has attacked this land—and not without reason. All the previous grand princes paid a yearly tribute to the Khan of the Crimea.[1] The present Grand Prince has been unwilling to give the Crimean Khan his fit tribute for the past few years. Your Imperial Roman Majesty also learns of the great damage inflicted by the Crimean Khan upon the Grand Prince and his country. If he, the Grand Prince, should reign a hundred years

---

[1] It is true that much of Russia was tributary to the Golden Horde until the second half of the fifteenth century; but any tribute (disguised as presents) that the Muscovite grand princes paid to the Crimean khans was exceptional and for specific purposes.

and more—which is, of course, impossible—even then he could not repair all the damage caused by the Crimean Khan to Moscow and the Ryazan land. Every year the Grand Prince must station his troops on the Oka River, fourteen miles from the city of Moscow, for the entire summer. Previously the troops of the Grand Prince met the Crimean Khan near the Don and the Donets, on the wild steppe between the Crimea and the Ryazan land. The Crimean Khan has devastated the Ryazan land. The Grand Prince keeps a number of harquebusiers there in wooden fortresses or castles. All the princes and boyars, as well as all the peasants in the Ryazan land, have been taken captive into the Crimea.

The Crimean Khan is so eager to conquer Russia that I cannot sufficiently write or tell your Imperial Roman Majesty about it; especially because the Turkish Sultan has set up Stephen Bathory as King of Poland just as he set up [the Khan] in the Crimea.

Thus, the Crimean Khan now strives to conquer Russia with the support and assistance of the Turkish Sultan —who does not deny him this support—to carry the Grand Prince and his two sons, bound, into captivity, and to seize the great treasure that has taken many centuries to collect. From this the Turkish Sultan would receive an especially large sum.

The Turkish Sultan has already ordered the Pyatigorskii Tatars,[2] who usually raid Lithuania and Poland and who caused great damage in Poland last year, to make a truce with Poland so that the Polish King would have a better opportunity to attack the troops of the Grand Prince. This is all to the advantage of the Crimean

[2] The Pyatigorskii Tatars were Circassian Tatars of the Caucasus region.

76

Khan, for at present the Grand Prince can offer no one a battle in the field. As soon as [the Grand Prince] sees that the army of the King of Poland is too strong for his own forces, he immediately has everything burned for a number of miles so that the King's army has no provisions or fodder. He does the same to the army of the King of Sweden. As soon as the forces of the kings of Poland and Sweden retreat, the Grand Prince immediately prepares his army and advances into Poland or Sweden, robbing and burning. Often, when he sees an advantage, the Grand Prince moves into Poland, Livonia, and Sweden, snatches a castle or two or three, and even a city, and immediately turns back to Moscow. At present he usually returns not to Moscow but to Aleksandrova Sloboda.

The Crimean Khan has the support of the Nogais, who have no ruler, and who usually serve the Grand Prince by freely raiding Poland, Lithuania, Livonia, and Sweden. He also has the support of the Grand Prince's [father-in-law] in the Circassian land, because the Grand Prince has treated his daughter unjustly and has had his son, Prince Mikhail, killed. He also has the support of the Tatars who live in the two khanates of Kazan and Astrakhan and of those, like the Lugovye and Nagornye Cheremisians, who live in the surrounding ulus—or districts. When the Crimean Khan burned down Moscow and devastated the Ryazan country, he had 30,000 Nogai horsemen with him. The Grand Prince's brother-in-law, Prince Mikhail Cherkasskii, was also with the Crimean Khan with a few thousand horsemen.[3] The Tatars of both the Kazan and Astrakhan khanates also rose. They

[3] Prince Mikhail was indeed Ivan's brother-in-law, but it was Mikhail's father who went to Moscow with the Crimean Khan.

robbed, burned, and murdered, and led several thousand Russians into their country as captives. These two khanates of Kazan and Astrakhan previously belonged to the Crimean Khan's cousin Shig-Alei. The fact that the King of Sweden as well as the Livonians were warring with the Grand Prince was also to the advantage of the Crimean Khan. That is not too important, however, because the Crimean Khan has sufficient support from the Turkish Sultan, the Nogai Tatars, Prince Mikhail [actually Temriuk] Cherkasskii, the Tatars of Kazan and Astrakhan, and the King of Poland. He does not have to depend on [the King of Sweden], unless he so chooses.

What the outcome of this shall be, and what its importance to all Christendom is, I leave for your Imperial Roman Majesty to decide, because your Imperial Roman Majesty is the head of the Christian world. So that [the Tatar conquest of Russia] is averted, so that it does not dishonor Almighty God, His Son Jesus Christ, and the Holy Ghost, and so that it does not diminish your Imperial Roman Majesty and bring the Christian world to utter ruin, but so that instead it may bring praise and honor to Almighty God, His Son Jesus Christ, and the Holy Ghost, and to your Imperial Roman Majesty, so that it may bring you the highest and greatest honor and riches, and so that it may be useful and edifying for the Christian world of which your Imperial Roman Majesty is the head, I give your Imperial Roman Majesty the following advice and plan.

An Unknown Passage or Way to Moscow by Water and Land

Pechenga is a monastery that was founded by a monk named Trifon, who went there from Great Novgorod 23 years ago by way of Norway and Vardöhus in Lapland. He and his monks and servants got their food from the sea. They caught cod and salmon and killed fish called beluga, from which they boiled train oil. They had a house in the Kola settlement and boiled salt from the Kola River.

Kildin is a high island that is washed by the sea and inhabited by Lapps. There is a fresh-water lake on the island.

Kola is a river or bay. The Russians, especially Iakov and Grigorii Anikeevich Stroganov, have built houses on this river, and within the past three years have also built a salt works.[4] These two brothers also own the cities of Velikaya Perm and Solvychegodsk. They trade on this river with Dutchmen, merchants from Antwerp, and others from overseas. They have promised the Grand Prince that they will fortify this place. Those from Holland and Antwerp have brought to this place several hundred bells that came from churches and monasteries, as well as all kinds of church ornaments, crowns, altar lamps, brass choir lattices, sacerdotal robes, censers, and many things of that type.[5]

At the Chernaya Reka [river] there is a bay where salmon are caught. A number [of merchants] from Kholmogory have the right to trade with the Lapps at this river.

Tersky Nos [the Kolsky Peninsula] is a land that stretches far into the sea. Lapps live there.

The Kandalaksha is a river where there is an unfortified settlement and a small monastery. These people, as

---

[4] Iakov and Grigorii Anikeevich Stroganov were members of Muscovy's foremost commercial family. They were instrumental in opening Siberia to Russian exploitation.

[5] Most likely this was booty from the Dutch War of Independence.

well as the monks and their servants, get their food from the sea. Lapland ends here.

The Umba and the Varzuga are rivers at which unfortified settlements have been built. Several thousand salmon are caught in one day during the summer on the Feast of St. John. Most of these salmon are sent to the household of the Grand Prince.

The Keret is a river and an unfortified settlement. The people there make their living from glass that is broken from the earth. It is torn into thin sheets and then windows are made from it. In Russian it is called *sliuda* [muscovite].

The Kem is a river. On this river there is a large unfortified settlement that supports itself by herring and salmon fishing.

Shuya in Karelia is a bay and an unfortified settlement. It was devastated by the oprichniki.

Solovetskii is a monastery, and lies on an island. It is washed on all sides by the sea, and one can sail around this small island in a ship. Six Russian princes have entered this monastery with all their money and property.

The Suma is a river or an unfortified settlement and belongs to that same Solovetskii monastery. It trades in many goods and boils train oil.

The Nimenga. There is a settlement on this river and the people boil salt from the sea. Beyond that lies the River Onega and then Zolotitsa and the Nikolaevskii monastery.

The [Northern] Dvina is a river. Along this river at the seacoast is an unfortified settlement called Kholmogory, to which the English travel. They have a trading company here in which there are about fifty of the richest merchants. The Queen [of England] is also in the company, which has a letter from the Grand Prince permitting it to come here every year with seven ships. No one else may sail to this place.

Beyond that lies Una Nunnuy.[6] In the sea lie seven islands, which elk run upon. Beyond that lies the River Mezen, and along the river is Lampozhnya; [then comes] the Tsilma River. There are exposed layers of silver ore here.

Beyond that lies Pustozersk. The Samoyeds and the Russians gather to trade here. The Russians trade broadcloth, kettles, bacon, butter, chain mail, and oat flour for the sables of the Samoyeds. Russian merchants come this far.

Beyond this the Grand Prince has no more territory, because the Russians do not go to sea. They have no ships and do not use the seas—neither the White Sea, nor the Baltic, nor the Caspian, nor the Black Sea. The land of the Grand Prince extends to all four of these seas.[7]

If one wants to penetrate inland, one must use the River Onega. Before the mouth of the river lies an island called Kii, which is washed all around by the sea. The Onega is a bay and a river. The first village on this river is named, in Russian, Prechistoye. Upstream from this village, merchants and peasants live on both banks up to Turchasov.

Turchasov is a large unfortified settlement. All the salt that is boiled from the sea is weighed here for the first time. The salt is then sent further up the Onega to Kargopol.

[6] No one is certain what "Una Nunnuy" means.

[7] The Muscovite dominions did not extend to the Black Sea; the Crimean Khan controlled a large seacoast area, as well as the Crimea itself.

Kargopol, an unfortified settlement without walls, lies by a stagnant lake on the high ground where the Onega River has its source. The storehouse for the salt that is boiled from the sea is here. Only merchants and peasants live in this city and in the entire area. Every year they pay the Treasury what they owe. None are troubled by the war or have anything to do with it.

One-half mile beyond this stagnant lake lies another stagnant lake called Beloye Ozero. There is a city here called Belozersk after the lake. The walls and fortifications are of wood. There is also a monastery called the Kirillo monastery in this region. One-half mile from here, there is a nunnery in which the princesses [wives] of the Grand Prince and his sons live. It is said that a great deal of the Grand Prince's treasure is in this city and monastery. Merchants and peasants live in this region.

Beyond this monastery it is sixteen miles to the city of Vologda. The city is just being built. [The lower] half of one wall is made of stone, the other half of wood. Within this city, there is a stone palace that contains silver and gold den'gi, jewels, and sables; for here is the storehouse for the sables that come from the Samoyeds and Siberia. About three hundred pieces of cannon that were recently cast in Moscow also lie in a pile here. Merchants and peasants live in this region. During the time of the oprichnina, five hundred harquebusiers used to stand watch in this city day and night.

Therefore, one can come to this country first by sea from Spain, France, Germany, Hamburg, Emden, Bremen, Holland, Zeeland, and Antwerp; then up the River Onega and the [Northern] Dvina. By land and by water, one can come to these four cities [Turchasov, Kargopol, Belozersk, and Vologda].

One can also go further by water to Moscow: from Belozersk by the River Sheksna, which flows from the stagnant lake Beloye Ozero into the large River Volga. Along the River Sheksna there are no cities or castles; but log dams are built in order to catch sturgeon that come from the Caspian and make their way to the stagnant lake Beloye Ozero. All these sturgeon are eaten at the court of the Grand Prince. At the point where the Sheksna flows into the Volga lies the unfortified settlement of Ustye. Further up the Volga lies a large settlement named Kholopii [Borisoglebskiye Slobody?] where there used to be a fair the year around. Turkish, Persian, Armenian, Bukharan, Shemakhan, Kizilbash, Siberian, Nogai, Circassian, German, and Polish merchants generally met here. Merchants from seventy Russian cities were registered, and had to come to this market every year.[8] The Grand Prince used to receive a large annual tariff here. At present the settlement is completely desolated. One can go further by water to the city of Uglich. This city is completely desolated. Beyond that lies the city of Dmitrov. This city is also desolated. One can come this far by water. Beyond that it is still twelve miles to the city of Moscow.

The way by land from these four cities: from Vologda to Rostov. Rostov is an unfortified city where there is a monastery. When the Crimean Khan burned Moscow, the Grand Prince hid in this monastery, because the monks find in their writings that no heathen enemy who

---

[8] The number seventy is certainly an exaggeration.

does not believe in Christ shall come to this place. Then to Yaroslavl. Yaroslavl is a city and castle built of wood and without guns. Beyond that is Pereyaslavl-Zalesski. This city and castle are completely desolated. Beyond that lies Aleksandrova Sloboda. This sloboda is built as follows: the walls are made of logs fitted together and filled with earth. To prevent fire, a brick wall around the outside of the wooden bulwark reaches from the ground up to the guns. A lot of money and property that the Grand Prince robbed from the cities of Tver, Torzhok, Great Novgorod, and Pskov is kept here. Further on lies a monastery called Troitskii, the richest monastery in the country. Beyond that lies the city of Moscow. It is presently built thus: the gates, likewise the citadel, are built of logs; around the outside of the logs there is sod and earth. Between the gates is a wall eighteen feet thick. There is no moat outside the walls. All those who live in the city are merchants, and have been assigned here from other cities, the richest ones against their wills. They had to spend their money building houses or courts. The [Moscow] River flows to the east and empties into the Oka. The Oka flows into the Volga, and the Volga empties into the Caspian. All the German soldiers that the Grand Prince used against the Crimean Khan live on the other side of the Yuza, in Bolvanovka.

The burned-out nunnery lies to the south. All the hunters and stableboys live to the west. All the German and Russian harquebusiers live to the north. Most of the German merchants who were removed from Livonia live in the city on the small river Neglinna, which was the border between the oprichnina and the zemshchina.

Taking, occupying, and holding this country will require two hundred well-supplied ships, two hundred

pieces of field artillery or iron gatlings, and 100,000 men
—not because one needs so many against the enemy, but
in order that the country may be occupied and held.[9]

The King of Denmark will certainly lend your Imperial Roman Majesty a hundred well-supplied ships,
along with munition, for this Christian enterprise. The
reason is that the Grand Prince has taken a number of
forts from him, and intends to take all of Norway as soon
as he makes peace with Poland. The Grand Prince has
also dealt with his brother Duke Magnus in a very un-
Christian manner.

The Hanse towns[10] and sea cities will readily lend your
Imperial Roman Majesty the other hundred ships. And
your Imperial Roman Majesty could request that the
Prince of Orange lend your Imperial Roman Majesty a
hundred ships for one trip. Or your Imperial Roman
Majesty can perhaps get a hundred ships in Spain or
France. The city of Hamburg would willingly lend your
Imperial Roman Majesty a number of ships for one trip.
The city of Bremen would also do something for this
[enterprise], likewise the city of Lübeck.[11]

The shipping costs or the initial sum required will be
100,000 talers. The troops must be equipped so that

---

[9] The absurdity of Staden's plan is first revealed in this passage. The
number of men, guns, and ships he specifies would not have been sufficient for such a task. And the Holy Roman Emperor was in no position to raise even the force Staden suggests.

[10] The Hanse towns were the members of a German mercantile
league, which had lost most of its political significance by the time
Staden wrote his account.

[11] Staden displays a total ignorance of the political condition of Europe at that time. He apparently did not know who was allied with
whom, and was unaware of the conflicting interests of the cities and
states he mentions.

when they arrive in the country they will also be able to serve on horseback.[12] They must be soldiers who have nothing to lose in the Christian world, neither house nor farm, and there certainly are enough of those in the Christian world. I have seen so many soldiers on the bum [*auf der garte gahn*] in the Christian world that more than one country could be conquered with them. If the Grand Prince had in his country the beggers who are on the bum in the Christian world, some stealing and being hanged, he would be able to conquer and occupy all the surrounding territory that now stands empty and without a sovereign.

A number of heavy cannons will also be needed in order to shoot down the gates of the wooden cities, and mortars to throw fire into the wooden cities and monasteries, should it be necessary.

Skippers and pilots will be found in Holland, in Zeeland, in Hamburg, and in Antwerp. At The Brill in Holland there are skippers and pilots, likewise at Dordrecht. In Schiedam there lives a skipper named Jacob Heine, who has sailed this coast for a number of years. A skipper named Johann Jacob, who has sailed to this place for a long time, lives in Antwerp. A man named Simon van Salingen lives in Hamburg; he has known this place a long while and is quite familiar with the Onega and the seacoast [I] described. Severin [and] Michael Falck live at Bergen in Norway; they found this place four years before I was there. They could travel in the ships that the King of Denmark will lend your Imperial Roman Majesty for one trip. In my opinion Hamburg would lend your Imperial Roman Majesty perhaps

[12] Notice that Staden does not describe the terrain or climate of northern Russia.

a hundred ships in order to acquire sailing rights to this land; for the King of Denmark will no longer permit the men of Hamburg to sail to Bergen in Norway and to Iceland.

Your Imperial Roman Majesty must choose one of your Imperial Roman Majesty's brothers to conquer and rule the country. He must not be strict at first and must readily talk with rich and poor and grant everyone friendly audiences until the country is taken. There must also be at least a hundred chaplains with the troops. In the entrenchments and cities, which will be fortified, they will teach the troops God's word correctly. They can certainly be found in the universities.

Everything must be arranged within one year so that everyone is ready when it is time to set sail from Germany —from Hamburg, Bremen, or Emden.

[One ought to set out] on April 1, and sail to the river and bay of Kola in Lapland. Kola is a strong point, for it lies between two rivers. One flows from Lake Ilmen. The other comes from Not Ozero and flows into the White Sea[13] here at Kola. Kola can be fortified and occupied with eight hundred men, half sailors and half harquebusiers. Then the island of Kildin must be fortified and garrisoned with five hundred men, half of them sailors. In this way all of Lapland can be guarded and defended for a hundred miles and more, both inland and along the coast. Then the Solovetskii monastery can be garrisoned with five hundred men, half of them sailors.

Those who resist and are taken prisoner should be transported to the Christian world in the same ships.

---

[13] *Westsehe.* This was the White Sea in Staden's understanding, actually the Barents Sea.

They must be shackled with irons and imprisoned in castles and cities. Or they can be put to work with their legs in irons welded with lead, until the country is taken, because they sell our prisoners to the Turks. What should be done with them afterward is indicated below.

One can set up a depot here. Then Kholmogory, an unfortified city on the seacoast, must be fortified, and garrisoned with eight hundred men. [To get to this city,] the English sail to the mouth of the [Northern] Dvina River. Then Kii, an island in the mouth of the Onega— or Prechistoye, a village on the Onega, a mile inland from the seacoast—must be fortified, and must be garrisoned with a thousand men. Thus, half of the sailors must garrison the seacoast.

With this [much taken], one holds more than three hundred miles of roads, land, and coast. A commissariat should be set up on this coast to procure by ship, from both inside and outside the country, all the goods needed in Russia, and also to deliver to Kargopol, [which lies] on very high ground, everything the field commander needs. It is possible, therefore, to bring in sufficient reinforcements from the Christian world every year. The Grand Prince cannot get reinforcements except by forcing his peasants into military service; but they are not armed, as are the peasants in the Christian world, and they know nothing about war.

It is necessary, therefore, to advance in barks and boats and also by land, as one chooses. One will then find an island lying in the Onega River near a waterfall. The salmon come from the sea this far—to fresh water. This island must be fortified and garrisoned—half horsemen, half foot soldiers. Only those who are armed should be killed. Never before has there been warfare in this place. All who live here are peasants and merchants. No one in these places has weapons. It [the island] lies three hundred miles from the court at Moscow.

For ten or twenty miles around every fort, the peasants and merchants should be registered in order that they may pay the soldiers and supply them with necessities. The captains must see, above all, that the troops supply the forts with everything—grain, salt, meat, and fish. Most important, all the best horses must be taken from the Russians, and all their barks, boats, and small ships must be brought together under the forts, so that everything can be defended with cannons.

One then comes to Turchasov, where the salt that is boiled from the sea is weighed for the first time. This unfortified city or settlement should be strengthened and garrisoned with a thousand men.

Then one comes to the unfortified city of Kargopol, which lies on high ground. Everything can be carried along by ship to the mouth of the Onega River. By ship one can carry cannons, and everything that is needed for war, to the unfortified city of Kargopol on the Onega River. In peacetime the Russians would customarily go downstream by bark from Kargopol into Norway or Denmark and again upstream by bark to the city of Kargopol. A commissariat must also be established in this city to send goods to the coast, and to receive what the field commander needs for war. This unfortified city must be strengthened and garrisoned with three thousand men. So far there is no danger that the enemy will appear.

One should then advance to Vologda, where the treasure lies. If it cannot be taken quickly, then one-third of the troops should be left outside the city. They can take the city and garrison it, and defend everything that is fortified and occupied—so that the Russians from behind or from the seacoast cannot reconquer any fort and thus

interrupt our passage to and from the country. In regard
to the treasure that lies in the stone palace, it can be de-
creed that nothing be pilfered from it.

Monasteries and churches must be off limits. Cities
and villages should be free booty for the soldiers.

And take the city called Belozersk—or White Lake—
along with the Kirillo monastery and the nunnery, for
the princesses of the Grand Prince and his sons are there.
Belozersk—or White Lake—must also be garrisoned
with three thousand men—one-half always foot soldiers
and the other half horsemen.

Ustye is the settlement that lies on the point where the
Sheksna flows into the Volga. This must also be fortified,
because three rivers come together here. One can therefore prevent anyone from traveling up or down the Volga. Garrison it with two thousand men. Then move forward and plunder Aleksandrova Sloboda, and garrison
the sloboda with two thousand men. Then plunder the
Troitskii monastery and afterward garrison it with one
thousand men, half of them horsemen.

If the enemy comes, line up in battle order. One should
see if it is possible to confer with a Russian; or a prisoner
can be sent to them to ask for a parley. The great tyranny
of the Grand Prince should then be set forth to [the Rus-
sians]. Our commander must be amiable and talk with
them and suggest that each [noble] send for the deed to
his estates. If they will willingly surrender, then he, the
commander, will sign the deed himself in their presence,
thereby protecting them. Now when the Russians see
that they face a long war, which can protect them
against the Grand Prince, and when they see that the
commander is so kind and affable, they will not turn this
[offer] down, but will desire it themselves.

From this account, your Imperial Roman Majesty can see what dire need Russia presently stands in. The Grand Prince has been such a grim and horrid tyrant that neither laymen nor clerics favor him, and all the neighboring sovereigns are his enemies, the heathens as well as the Christians. All this is at present impossible to describe. Yet if it is not possible [to win over the Russian nobility], one must do what one can. I know for certain that no bloodletting will be necessary. The army of the Grand Prince can no longer give battle to anyone in the open field.

Volokolamsk, beyond [the Troitskii monastery], must be garrisoned with a thousand men. It lies fifteen miles from Moscow. Volokolamsk is a neglected, unfortified city. There is a stone church that should be filled with provisions and other war supplies. A mile from there lies Osipov, a monastery rich in money and goods. One can plunder it and take [the money and goods] off to the castle. Then Zvenigorod must be garrisoned. After the conquest of Kazan, it was given to the Khan of Kazan, Shig-Alei,[14] for his maintenance. This city and the castle stand unfortified and should be garrisoned with two thousand men. The city lies eight miles from Moscow. The small city of Kolomna must be taken. It also should be garrisoned with fifteen hundred men. Then the burned-out nunnery that lies one-half mile from Moscow should be garrisoned with fifteen hundred men. Beyond that the Grand Prince's burned-out summer house at Kolomenskoe, a mile east of Moscow, should be garrisoned with fifteen hundred men. Then Bolvanovka, where the German soldiers live, can be fortified and

---

[14] It was actually given to Derbysh-Alei, former khan of Astrakhan.

garrisoned with two thousand men. Then the place where all the German and Russian harquebusiers live must be fortified and garrisoned with fifteen hundred men. These settlements lie a quarter mile from Moscow. One can set up camp around these, and at the same time fortify and garrison them. Then no one can take anything into or out of Moscow. Thus, the city of Moscow can be won without a shot's being fired.

I do not think it will be necessary to fortify too much. When the Russians realize that an army is staying in the country winter and summer, they will see that they can be protected from the Grand Prince.

The Grand Prince will quickly withdraw to a city. Now it is obvious that he does not have a strong city in his country. They are all well known to me. Most of the monasteries, and [certainly] the richest ones, have stone walls. The cities and forts of the country are built of logs filled with earth. In the center of the country all the cities and forts are neglected and desolate. The Grand Prince has preserved only Kazan and Astrakhan and the border posts and cities near Poland, Livonia, and Sweden. He is not at all concerned about the place I described. And no one from our country who has been in Moscow or visited the Grand Prince has either heard of or seen the places I described.

When the Grand Prince retreats into a city, he must be besieged. When his own Russians see that [the campaign] only concerns the Grand Prince, then one can soon have their support. The true military leaders have all been killed.

When the Grand Prince is captured, the treasure should be taken to the Holy Roman Empire of his Imperial Roman Majesty Rudolf, and should be deposited in his treasury. It is pure gold, which has been put away from year to year by the previous grand princes, together with all their crowns, scepters, and raiment; [it includes] all the remarkable treasures that the deceased grand princes have assembled, along with those the present Grand Prince has justly and unjustly brought together —which is a great deal. Silver money and cannons and everything pertaining to war may remain in the country.

Then the Grand Prince and his sons should be led, bound as prisoners, through their own land and to the Christian world. When the Grand Prince is brought to the border of the Christian world, he should be met with thousands of horses, and should then be led with his sons to the high ridge where the Rhine or Elbe originates. Then all the Russian prisoners from his country should be brought there and killed in the presence of [the Grand Prince] and his two sons so that he and his sons see it with their own eyes. The corpses should then be tied together by the ankles. A log should be taken and placed between the legs of the corpses so that thirty, forty, or even fifty can hang on each log, as many as the log can bear in the water without sinking. The corpses with the logs should then be thrown into the water and floated [downstream], so the Grand Prince will see that no one should rely upon his own power and that his prayers and religious services are a sin; for the Grand Prince prays to God through St. Nicholas and other dead saints. And those of us who say we are Christians may reflect and learn from this too, and they may strengthen and reinforce their belief in God the Father, Son, and Holy Ghost, and may trust them [sic] and place hope only in Jesus Christ, the Almighty Son of God, through God the Holy Ghost and believe, trust and pray to Him alone. The Grand Prince and his sons should be given an earldom in some suitable place in the Christian world. When he has viewed this spectacle, he and his two sons should be taken to this earldom and guarded, but in a way that they may stand, ride, or walk [freely] in this earldom. Two or three preachers should be assigned to properly teach him the word of God daily. Perhaps the Russian scriptures can be translated and collated with ours. He will then realize that our scriptures are true. Because he conquered Livonia, he asserts that he serves God properly and that our religious practice is untrue.

In Russia neither Latin, Hebrew, nor Greek is learned or used by the metropolitan, the bishops, the monks, the priests, the princes, the boyars, the clerks, or the scribes. They use only their own language and know no other. Yet the simplest peasant is so practiced in roguishness that he is more cunning and cautious than our doctors who have studied law. When one of our most learned doctors arrives in Moscow, he must study again from the beginning.

As soon as this country is taken, then Poland belongs to the Roman Empire. When the land is taken, it can then be divided into two or three parts, as one wishes, for the country is large—six hundred miles long and wide. If one travels from Kola, in Lapland, to Astrakhan, on the Caspian Sea, one will realize this. A trip from Polotsk or Ozerishche, in Poland, to Pustozersk, where the Samoyeds meet with the Russians to trade bacon and oats, will show the same.

In order that the land may be well governed, the soldiers should be granted estates in the country immediately, each according to his service. And they should [return to the army] from time to time, when it is necessary. The ruler of the country must also have the word of God preached to our people. In every village, next to the Russian church, which is small and built of wood, our kind of church must also be built, of stone or of wood. Our churches will then remain standing, while the Russian churches will be neglected. In Russia, in my estimation, there are more and not less than 10,000 deserted churches, in which no Russian services are celebrated. Several thousand have rotted away.

The ruler of the country must see to it that people are found to repopulate the Ryazan region; for this land is the gateway to Russia and to the city of Moscow. I have never seen a land as beautiful as Ryazan. When a peasant plants three or four bushels of grain, he has enough to do just to harvest it. The land is fertile. All the manure is taken to the river so that when the snow melts and the river rises, the manure is washed away. There are a great many linden trees in the land, which are filled with bees and honey. In all, it is a beautiful land. Most of the farmsteads are empty. Others have been burned down. The sovereign of Russia can seize the lands around here that have no ruler, and can settle the empty lands.

It must be arranged that a special sum of money, collected annually from all the conquered lands, be sent to the Emperor of the Holy Roman Empire, Rudolf. The kings of Sweden and Denmark must also annually give a set sum of money to the Emperor of the Holy Roman Empire, Rudolf; and likewise the Queens of England and Scotland. The reason is this: Russia lies northeast of England, and Spain lies beneath [England]. If the Queen will not do this, she must avoid Russia and Spain, and cannot profit from them.

When Russia and the surrounding lands that lie empty

and without a ruler are taken, then one is at the borders of the Shah of Persia. Only then will the Turkish Sultan see how God the Almighty fights for those who firmly believe in His Son and trust Him wholeheartedly.

It is also possible to reach America and [advance] into it from the surrounding lands.

Then one can quite easily deal with the Turkish Sultan with the support of the Shah of Persia.

IV. [*Staden's Autobiography*]

In this next part and description one learns how I, Heinrich von Staden, went to Livonia and from there to Moscow, how I stayed there with the Grand Prince, and how the merciful God then saved me from the hands and power of those non-Christians and brought me back to Germany.

I, Heinrich von Staden, the son of a burgher, was born in the city of Ahlen, which is in the bishopric of Münster, and is one mile from Beckum, three miles from the city of Münster, one mile from Hamm, and two miles from Warendorf.[1] Many of my relatives, the von Stadens, live in the city of Ahlen and in other neighboring towns.

My father was a simple, good, pious, and honorable man who was called Old Walter, because my cousin Walter von Staden was called The Younger. The latter is presently mayor of Ahlen. My father, however, has peacefully passed on to God the Almighty with a happy expression and a smile on his lips. My mother's name was Kattarina Ossenbach. She died during the plague. They lived in the first house on the right, as one goes into the city by the east gate. Three houses are built as one. My

---

[1] Staden was perhaps born in 1545.

late parents dwelt there as befits a pious Christian married couple. My sister now lives in the same house, and is married to a nobleman named Johann von Galen. My brother, Herr Bernhardus von Staden, is the pastor in Untrop and the vicar in Ahlen.[2]

When I had studied in Ahlen long enough that I could plan to become a priest, an unexpected accident occurred: at school I was accused of stabbing a student in the arm with an awl. As a result our parents sued each other.

Meanwhile, my cousin Steffan Hovener, a citizen of Riga, arrived from Livonia. He said to me, "Cousin, come with me to Livonia. You will not be disturbed there."

As we went through the city gate [on the way to Livonia], my brother-in-law, Franz Baurmann, a city councilor, was with us. He took a thorn bush and said, "I must wipe out the track so that Heinrich von Staden will not soon find the way back again."

In Lübeck I stayed at the house of my cousin Hans Hovener. He sent me with a wheelbarrow to work on the [city] walls, where I had to wheel earth. Every evening I had to turn in my work slip [to my cousin] so that none would be missing when he demanded payment.

Six weeks later I sailed with my cousin to Riga in Livonia. There I was in the service of Philip Glandorf, a city councilor and a strict man. I had to work on the walls again. It was awfully hard work. Because the Grand Prince was advancing, the walls had to be put up quickly [1560]. The distributor of the work marks then became ill, and he entrusted me with his job. I secured so many

---

[2] "Untrop," spelled "Untorp" on old maps, lies just south of the Lippe River, about five miles east of Hamm.

A group of Ivan IV's noblemen.

work marks for myself that I did not have to work on the walls any longer. So I simply walked back and forth on the walls and looked things over. I therefore learned how a wall should be laid or built. My cousin Steffan Hovener then said to me, "You are a ne'er-do-well." I therefore ran away, and went to the city of Wolmar [Valmiera].

Here I found work with the bailiff Heinrich Müller and had to learn Livonian farm procedure. I was often flogged with rods, and therefore I ran away and went to the Wolgarten estate.

The noblewoman there asked me, "Can you read and write?" "I can read and write Latin and German," I answered. Her bailiff, George Junge, was dishonest. She therefore said to me, "I will trust you with all my estates. The stewards will instruct you. Be honest with me and I will look after you well." "But I am not more than seventeen or eighteen years old," I replied. I then became bailiff on the Wolgarten estate, the Patkull estate, Mellepen, and Udren. The nobleman Johann Bockhorst [the owner of these estates], who had been the richest in the country, was dead.

Thank God I knew that non-German [Latvian] language well, and I still do. George von Hochrosen came and married this widow, and took her with him to Hochrosen. The cousin of Johann Bockhorst then arrived from Germany, and inherited the estates.

I moved on, became a merchant, and went to the fortress of Karkus, where George Wolsdorf was commander. Karkus, Helmet, Ermes, Trikaten, Rujen, and Burtneck belonged at that time to Duke John of Finland, the present King of Sweden.[3] Then some soldiers with false papers came to Karkus and drove George Wolsdorf out. I lost my possessions at the same time, and I went to Helmet.

Count Johann von Arz had his court here. He had been appointed by the Duke to govern these six fortresses. He, however, conspired with the Grand Prince,

[3] Karkus, presently called Karksi, is now part of the town of Nuia in the southern Estonian S.S.R., about eighteen miles south of Vilyandi.

Helmet was about twelve miles further south-southeast.

Ermes, in what is now the Latvian S.S.R., was about 45 miles south of Vilyandi.

Trikaten, also in the present Latvian S.S.R., was about twelve miles east of Valmiera.

Rujen, presently called Rujiena, is about 25 miles north of Valmiera.

Burtneck was located about twelve miles north-northwest of Valmiera, on the southeast shore of Lake Burtnieki.

Helmet, Ermes, Trikaten, and Burtneck are probably small villages around castle ruins today. My information is from *Stielers Handatlas*, ed., H. Haack (Gotha, 1925).

and was therefore arrested and taken to Riga, where he was torn with hot tongs and executed. I witnessed this execution.

I then went with one horse to Prince Aleksandr Polubenski, the commander in Wolmar. He continually raided the bishopric of Dorpat with Polish soldiers, and we often captured Russian boyars along with their money and possessions. The booty was divided unequally, so I did not want to give up what I had taken. I was therefore taken into the city and thrown into prison, and they threatened to hang me.

To be brief, having seen enough of the Livonian government, which was ruining Livonia, and realizing with what cunning and craftiness the Grand Prince was taking the country, I ran away and came to the border. I had to worry about the hangman here, too, because all those who were deserting to the Grand Prince and were caught at the border were killed, and so were their entire families. Likewise, those from Livonia who wanted to join the Grand Prince were hanged if they were caught. The important people of Livonia were now going over to Moscow and serving the Grand Prince.

At the border, I stuck a pen in my hatband and put a piece of clean paper and an inkpot inside my shirt, so that I could make a plea if I was caught. When I crossed the border, the Embach [Ema River], I went to a nearby village and wrote to Joachim Schröter in Dorpat.[4] He was to make inquiries of the Grand Prince's commander. I was prepared to serve the Grand Prince if he would pay me; otherwise I would go to Sweden, but I needed an answer soon. The commander sent a boyar, Atalyk Kvashnin, to me with eight horses. He received me in a

[4] Dorpat was held by the Russians.

friendly way and said, "You will get everything from the Grand Prince that you ask."

When I came to the commander, Prince Mikhail Morozov, at the castle in Dorpat, he received me in a friendly manner and said, "If you wish to serve the Grand Prince, we will give you estates in his name. You know conditions in Livonia and its language." "No," I said, "I want to see the Grand Prince." "Where in Poland is the King now?" he then asked me. "I have never been in Poland," I answered.

A post horse and a boyar were ready. I went from Dorpat to Moscow, covering the two hundred miles by stages in six days.

I was taken to the Chancellery for Ambassadors, and questioned about various things by the clerk Andrei Vasilievich. All this was written down at once for the Grand Prince. Very soon I was given a pamiat' or chit. With this I could demand and get a quart-and-a-half—or a pail—of mead, and four den'gi allowance, at the post station every day. At the same time I was given a silk caftan, cloth for clothes, and a coin as a present.

When the Grand Prince came to Moscow, I was brought before him as he was going from the church to the palace. The Grand Prince laughed and said, "Khleba est'," and with these words he invited me to dine. Then I was given a pamiat' or chit in the Land Chancellery. I received the estate of Tesmino with all its villages. It had belonged to Andrei Kholopov, Prince Vladimir's treasurer. Duke Magnus has [married] Prince Vladimir's daughter.

I began at the top. The Grand Prince knew me, and I knew him. I began to study. I already knew the Russian language fairly well.

There were only four of us Germans in the court of the Grand Prince's oprichnina—two Livonian noblemen, Johann Taube and Elert Kruse,[5] I, Heinrich von Staden, and Caspar Elverfeld, who had been an official at Petershagen in Germany and was a doctor of law. The hearts of the two Livonian noblemen always longed for the kingdom of Poland. They eventually managed to get to King Sigismund August with all their possessions, wives, and children. The King gave Johann Taube the farmstead Karallen in Livonia, and Elert Kruse got Treyden on the river Aa.[6] They both lost their estates through pride, but the present King, Stephen, gave them estates again, although they never saw the Kargopol-Sheksna seacoast that I described. Johann Taube was given several thousand acres in Lithuania in a place not far from the city of Kovno, and Elert Kruse got as much on the Prussian border; and they never thought of the project I described.

Caspar Elverfeld and I turned our hearts toward the Roman Empire. Elverfeld had been with the Grand Prince at the oprichnina court before I arrived. When he saw that I lived in the zemshchina and made a lot of money by keeping a tavern, he decided to get my money in the following way. He took a chest or box and had a

---

[5] Johann Taube and Elert Kruse were Livonian noblemen who were captured by the Russians early in the Livonian war. Beginning in the middle 1560's, they served Ivan IV in diplomatic capacities, and participated with Duke Magnus in the siege of Reval in 1570–71, after which they defected to Sigismund August. Taube and Kruse wrote an account of their experiences in Russia: "Sendschreiben an Gotthard Kettler, Herzog zu Kurland und Semgallen, 1572," which was printed in *Sammlung russischer Geschichte*, X, Part 1 (Dorpat, 1816), pp. 185–238.

[6] "Oka" in the manuscript. This is obviously wrong. Epstein and Polosin both suggest the River Aa, now the Gauya.

hole cut in the bottom.[7] He then put some clothes and other things in it, and had it put on a sled. He had some horses harnessed to the sled and sent it with two of his servants to my house. They drank at my tavern. He, however, rode off to the Law Court and petitioned the judge, saying that his servants had run away and had stolen several thousand talers from him. Now he knew where they were, and he wanted the witnesses and officials to return them, as was just. In Russia all worldly people take great joy in such things. When he came to my place, dressed very strangely, the witnesses and officials found the sled, servants, and horses. They were all cheerful, but he preferred to be high-handed. With vexation he climbed the stairs, thinking I was in the upper story. Here my servant Albrecht met him with a club, intending to bash in his head; but he said, "I am Caspar Elverfeld." When my servant heard this he refrained [from hitting him]. A witness or an official then seized and bound my steward, and took him off to the court, together with [Elverfeld's] servants, sled, and horses. The chest was tied up, and everything in it was likewise taken to court with the officials and [Elverfeld's] servants. Here he began to complain, "Sir, these servants of mine stole two thousand rubles from me and took them to this man's house—where, in the presence of these witnesses, I found them. Give me back my money!" "I do not have your money," [Albrecht] answered. "Your master keeps a tavern where people are murdered," [Elverfeld] said. "Permit me," my steward replied, "just as I am, to take you to [Elverfeld's] house. There I will show you that in the cellar or under the floor lie dead bodies." [Elverfeld] then grew despondent, and

[7] It is not clear why he cut the hole.

the gentlemen [of the court] became gay. When I learned of this, I was not at all frightened, for I knew that [Albrecht] would win. I quickly rode off to this affair and came before the court myself. I got up and said to the gentlemen, "Here I am. Let my steward go!" [Elverfeld] looked at me crossly, but I was friendly. "Settle things between yourselves," the gentlemen said to both of us. "I shall do that," I answered. Herewith my steward was acquitted and set free.

I rode with [Elverfeld] to his house, where I made my proposal. I knew very well that because I lived in the zemshchina I would lose everything, for everyone who served the Grand Prince in the oprichnina had taken an oath not to speak with anyone from the zemshchina. It often happened that if two such men were found together, they were killed, whether they were of high or low rank. That is just, since they had sworn to their master by God and the cross, and in such cases God, not the master, would punish. I spoke up and said, "Good sir and countryman, I kindly ask you to take as much from me as you wish, and to remain my lord and countryman." "What do you want to give me?" he asked. "Two hundred rubles," I replied. He was satisfied with that. I then said that I presently had no money. "Give me a note," he answered, "and I will give you a year to pay." I then wrote the note and gave it to him in a friendly way.

We rode back to the Law Court. We thanked the gentlemen and he said to them, "I have been paid." I then paid the court costs, as is usual, and he rode back to his house and I to mine. He was happy, and I was not sad; he was thinking of getting the money, and I was wondering how I might have him strangled.

Duke Magnus then came to Moscow. Johann Taube

was there at the same time. These two[8] were also enemies because Johann Taube told the Grand Prince that he [Taube] wanted to win Livonia with kindness. [Elverfeld] said that this was impossible, that it must be taken with force.

Johann Taube and Elert Kruse enjoyed great favor with the Grand Prince. [Elverfeld], however, was in disfavor. He now made me a considerable offer, and quite affably requested me to arrange for him to meet Johann Taube at some secluded place. I persuaded Johann Taube to come to my house in the oprichnina. They both met here in a new room and became friends once again.

Then he gave me a receipt. Now I had a lot of loyal people around me, and [Elverfeld] saw with his own eyes that I had carried on a lot of important business for the Grand Prince. Then I said to him in a loud voice, "Caspar Elverfeld! I was of a mind to have you killed somehow, on a dark night in the square by your house near the Law Court, as you came riding from the oprichnina court, because you have dealt with me in such an unChristian manner." These words stabbed this great, rich man, who had studied law, straight to the heart—so hard that he became clearly despondent and could not say a word. Obviously shaken, he stood up and had to go to prison in great shame.[9]

Afterward I visited him in prison. He then offered

---

[8] Epstein suggests Taube and Elverfeld. Polosin believed Staden meant Taube and Duke Magnus. The context indicates that Epstein was most probably correct, although the passage contains many pronouns without clear antecedents and no positive interpretation is possible.

[9] It is not clear why he should go to prison.

me everything he possessed to do with as I wished. He also authorized me, and the now-deceased Adrian Kalb, to go in his place to the English warehouse and demand his trunks, which he, fearing fire, had sent to Kholmogory to be stored in a cellar. When I went there they did not refuse to let me have them, and everything was brought to Adrian's place. I did not find his doctorate papers. The chests and boxes were clumsily secured. Adrian Kalb and I opened up and inspected everything that was there. We took everything to him and he saw that it was all properly accounted for. He then said, "My dear countrymen, go and sell everything and give what you wish for my maintenance in prison." I refused to do this.

During the time of the plague, when the Grand Prince saw that Duke Magnus and Johann Taube did not wish to accomplish anything by force, he sent a boyar by stage to Moscow to take Caspar Elverfeld to some place unaffected by the plague. In the meantime, God sent the plague to him, and he died and was buried in a court. I then asked one of the chief boyars in the oprichnina for permission to disinter the body in order to bury it in the crypt that the deceased had built of brick beforehand. It lay outside the city in the suburbs, where all Christians, German and foreign, were buried. Nalcka Peter Zeuze answered, "When the plague is over, that will be possible."

The Grand Prince had a letter given to me that said I, my servants, and my peasants were exempted from lawsuits brought by Russians, except on Christmas and on the Feast of Saints Peter and Paul; and [the Russians] would be cautious even then.

I lived most of the time in Moscow. Every day I was with the Grand Prince at court. I did not agree, how-

ever, to the suggestion made by the clerk Osip Il'in that
I should always stay with the Grand Prince. At that time
I was young and did not know Germany. If a gentleman
would ask my servant a question and receive a false answer, one can well imagine the anger of the gentleman
and the shame of the servant. Whoever was close to the
Grand Prince became scorched, and whoever was distant
froze.

Because of time, I have not been able to write any
more.[10]

When the Grand Prince took Staritsa into the oprichnina [in late 1569], he placed me on an equal level with
the princes and boyars of the fourth degree. The former
estates of the princes Menshik and Rudok Obolenskii, all
their votchiny and pomestia, were added to my other
estates. The villages of Krasnoye and Novoye were
votchiny, and six villages were pomestia. In addition, I
had a yearly income in proportion to the number of my
estates. The Grand Prince gave me a house in Moscow.
A priest formerly lived there. He had been taken prisoner in Polotsk and sent to the city of Vladimir. This house
was excluded from the municipal records, and was painted white because it was free of civil obligations.

Beside this house was another, inhabited by a German,
Johann Söge, who was a servant of the deceased Master
[of the Livonian Order] Wilhelm Fürstenberg. I had
loaned him my yearly allowance, and with it he bought
the house next to mine. He had a wife born in Dorpat,
who had been led off to Moscow. Since I had no legal
wife, this woman, to her advantage, served drinks in my

---

[10] This curious statement suggests that Staden's autobiography was
a diary or collection of notes, which was appended to his proposal to
Emperor Rudolf.

absence, especially when I was with the Grand Prince on campaign. She contributed more than once to the prohibition against foreigners operating taverns. When prikazchiki or officials from the Zemskii Dvor came to that woman's place, sealing her cellar and arresting everyone found drinking there, the woman said that they ought to go over to my place, and asked why they did not go to her neighbor's house. The officials, however, knew quite well what the word oprichnina meant. The man and woman learned it as well. My neighbors sold their place to me and bought another inside the city where the gates could be closed. I, however, had the two houses made into one, and received a crowd from the surrounding area day and night.

During the plague this neighbor of mine died and his wife and the wife of Lorensen, a master barber, wanted to leave Moscow in a covered wagon. This was stupid, because all the surrounding suburbs had been set afire by order of the Crimean Khan [in 1571]. As the wagon came to the gates, the fire got out of hand, and it burned along with the horses and all the jewels, gold, and silver that were in it. After the fire there was nothing to be found of the wagon but the metal parts. The gates were blocked with stones.

On Lubyansk Street, at the large Stretensk Street, just across from my house there was another house that was also painted white. A Pole from Polotsk had lived there but had been removed to another place. I acquired this house from a gentleman, Semen Kurtsov, who was the Grand Prince's falconer. During my time [in Moscow] the Grand Prince violated neither the one nor the other [house's immunity]. I gave this house to a German named Hans Kupferschmidt. He said he knew something about hydraulic machines. When he saw that there was a lot of money in tavern keeping, he decided that my business was better than his. When someone wanted to come with barrels and jugs, etc. to my place to buy mead, beer, or brandy, he sat in his window and waved them into his court. He could then expect more from them than I, and this caused me great damage.

I had this house of mine dismantled and moved to my other one near the small river Neglinna, where I had two empty houses built as one; it was not yet fenced in. Here I again began selling beer, mead, and brandy. The commoners in the oprichnina accused me in the law court of setting up a tavern. Grigorii Griaznoi was the judge and chief boyar at the Zemskii Dvor. He said he loved me as his own son, and his love produced money, rings, pearls, and suchlike. He rode about and inspected the fire guard and the watch houses, and said to the community, "This house belongs to a German who is a foreigner without kinfolk. If he did not keep a tavern, how would he fence in his house? And the fence must run up to the fire guard if it is to be correct."

In the zemshchina I had still another house that had belonged to a Livonian nobleman, Fromhold Hahn. At first he was taken prisoner in Livonia, but he got free, converted to Russian Orthodoxy, and was given the name Elias. He was then settled at the castle of Helmet in Livonia. Afterward he came to Moscow with me. When the Grand Prince ordered that estates be given to us, and the treasurer Ivan Viskovatyi asked him if we were brothers, he said "Yes." It was then determined that I should receive fifty morgens of land more than he, because I was the eldest. He thereupon replied that I was the son of a burgomaster and he the son of a nobleman.

He was then compensated [with land] as I. Thereupon our brotherly relationship came to an end.

This is how I proceeded in my affairs. I had a petition sent to the Grand Prince requesting a house as though I wanted a residence. On the same day I was assigned two empty houses. Of them I chose the priest's house mentioned above, and gradually began to sell drinks.

I was then constantly with the chief boyar Ivan Petrovich Cheliadnin, and was helping a Pole translate a German herbal book into Russian, because [Cheliadnin] loved it and was very enthusiastic about it. The gentleman went with me to the Land Chancellery and ordered the clerk Vasilii Stepanovich to give me the estate that I had requested, and he remained at the chancellery until the order was signed.

A nobleman named Evert Bremen, from Harrien or Wierland[11] [in Livonia], arrived [in Moscow], and could not get ahead because he had married, only by virtue of his nobility, a woman who had been expelled from Polotsk. I sent him to my estate to oversee my peasants according to instructions I wrote in German and Russian. He, however, managed the peasants according to Livonian practice, disregarding my instructions, and my estate was ruined. I then said to the aforementioned Semen Kurtsov, a lover of such birds as falcons and eagles, "Ride with me and this fellow to the Military Chancellery."

Everything that [Bremen] said was secretly written down. When he first arrived, he had gone to the wrong chancellery. He should have gone to the Chancellery for Ambassadors—that would have been correct—because

[11] Harrien and Wierland were old German territorial divisions. They were located along the Estonian coast on the Finnish Gulf.

German and Tatar affairs are dealt with there. At the
Military Chancellery all military and Polish affairs are
dealt with. This Semen Kurtsov immediately had a
pamiat'—or chit—drawn up, as is usual. It was written
according to the circumstances. First, with regard to their
language, *leto* means *anno* in Russian usage. Since they
number the years from the beginning of the world, they
write leto 7,000 and a few hundred. Then the text: "Nikita Funikov, you should treat this newly arrived German equally with his peers." Then followed the month
of the year and then the day. The clerk then wrote his
name right next to the date. This pamiat' remained at
the State Treasury. All the chits were glued up and
wound into a roll. At the State Treasury a pamiat' was
written: "Putilo Mikhailovich and Vasilii Stepanovich,
by command of the Grand Prince, give this newly arrived German 150 chetverts of land in the Muscovite
towns or districts that are not empty." This pamiat' remained in the Land Chancellery.

When the Grand Princess was poisoned,[12] the Grand
Prince sent to Livonia for a widow, named Katrina Schil-
ling, who lived in the city of Dorpat. This woman was
brought in a gilded wagon. The Grand Prince hoped
that she would be able to help the Grand Princess. He
examined the woman's clothes very closely and then said
to her, "If you help my empress, we will give you half
the income of the bishopric of Dorpat in Livonia for the
rest of your life." The Grand Princess said to the woman, "You can certainly help me. Help me!" The Grand
Princess died [1560], and the woman was sent back to

[12] Staden probably refers to the death of Anastasia Romanovna,
which occurred before he arrived in Russia.

Livonia. Later, when the Grand Prince had the Livonians removed from the captured cities, only this woman,
her daughter and sister from Wesenberg, and her brother were led to Moscow. The Grand Prince ordered that
a house in Moscow be given to this woman. The Grand
Prince sent Johann Taube to Livonia to win Duke Magnus over to him. Johann Taube requested that he be permitted to take this woman, with her daughter, sister, and
brother, back to Livonia with him. This woman gave me
her house and all her furniture, because I was a friend
of her daughter. This woman now lives with her daughter in Riga in Livonia.

I placed my servant Albrecht in this house, and he was
to keep a tavern there for half [of the profits]. I gave
him a deed of purchase as though I had sold the house to
him. Since I lived in the oprichnina, he thought "I have
the bill of sale and with it I can pressure my master and
resist him." I had a true friend, named Adrian Kalb, who
was a Livonian nobleman. We had an agreement by
which one would be the heir of the other in case of death.
[Kalb] rode to the house against my wishes and knowledge, grabbed [Albrecht] by the head, took the deed
from him, threw him out the door, and lived in the house
against my will. Taking his money, Adrian Kalb tried to
get away, and died from the plague on the way. He was
buried alongside the road. His son sent the money on to
Livonia. Johann Taube delivered it. I could not get the
money, because the road was barred on account of the
pestilence.

Then Fromhold Hahn, who was my friend and had
come with me to Moscow from Livonia, undertook the
following scheme. He had a petition drawn up and he
sent it to Grigorii Lokurov in the State Treasury. In the

petition he asked to be baptized a Russian Orthodox. It is a great joy to the great men of Moscow when a foreigner is baptized and takes their religion. They usually assist [in this] diligently, because they maintain that they are the holiest Christians on earth. They generally become godfathers themselves, and give christening gifts and gold brocade from the Treasury, and are helpful in every way.

While he was staying for six weeks in the monastery where he was taught how to practice their faith, as is the custom, he sent me a request. He wanted me to send him a German Lutheran book. I could not refuse him that. When he left the monastery, however, he got only a small gift for his christening, because he did not have the sense to ask the right boyar to be his sponsor. Afterward he was seized on his own land and brutally beaten by his neighbors, the boyars, with whom he had some absurd business. He continued to live on his land. When he had ruined his estate, he thought he would get another. He was unsuccessful, however, because those who want to do that need money. If one wants to bake a pie, it is necessary to smear the pan with butter, otherwise it will stick or burn. Another means can be used, if one has good connections, but one must be clever.

He was not permitted in our society, because he was baptized in the Russian faith. Since he had no place to stay, he was vexed. He therefore asked the Grand Prince to take him into the oprichnina, referring to me as a comrade. The Grand Prince sent to ask me if that was actually true. I testified that it was. The Grand Prince then gave him an estate in the Rzheva Volodimirova [Rzhev] district and he thus entered the oprichnina.

Then the Grand Prince, as already mentioned, went

and plundered his own people, land, and cities. I accompanied him with one horse and two servants. Because every city and road was guarded by soldiers, I could not get away with horses or servants. I finally returned to my estate with 49 horses, 22 pulling sleighs full of goods, which I sent to my house in Moscow.

[Hahn], learning of this, gathered all his servants and peasants when I was in Moscow, and came to my estate. He took everything there by force, even all the spring corn and grain. I heard of this when I was in Moscow. I cleverly set off at once with one servant, and came upon him at his estate so unexpectedly that he did not have time to put on a helmet before he had to explain to me. I settled the business by borrowing a sum of money for a period. I thereby got what was mine. He had to borrow bread from my place when he wanted to eat during the famine.

I exchanged his former estate with Johann Taube for the village of Spitsyno, which lies one mile from Moscow. This village had been assigned to Vorobevo, a podkletnoe selo of the Grand Prince, and was sold with the approval of the Grand Prince's brother-in-law, Nikita Romanovich. This place was for recreation. I kept horses in this village so I would have them on hand when I needed them. I continued to live on my estate in the oprichnina.

I kept the first estate in the zemshchina. There I had a maid who had been captured by the Tatars in Livonia. I trusted her with everything I had. Since it was often said that she stole from me, I replaced her and entrusted my affairs to a Tatar named Rudock. In my absence he behaved badly, destroying my property for no purpose. I commanded that he be punished, and he was stripped naked and whipped. The maid then took care of everything again. When [Rudock] learned of this, he had a copy of my key made for himself. I had another servant, a Livonian called Jacob. He was to keep [Rudock] prisoner. The Tatar persuaded him to let him go during the night. He then took the key and stole gold, pearls, precious stones, and jewels from me, and they both ran away. Later, when I wanted to give my mistress a piece of jewelry, I found the cache empty.

Not long afterward, I learned that these two servants of mine were sitting in jail in Pereyaslavl [-Zalesski]. They said that they had intended to go into a monastery with the goods. I petitioned the Grand Prince and begged for justice; but when I reached the town official [in Pereyaslavl-Zalesski] they had already been sent to Moscow together with the goldsmiths and merchants who had bought the stuff from them. They were guarded so closely that I could not talk with them. In Moscow I demanded justice. I did not forget to make the sum large enough, for the evidence was sealed for the court. The pearls and jewels that had been set in gold were gone. The gold and silver had been melted down. But there was enough evidence. Nothing could help the goldsmiths now. The princes and great boyars were not permitted to take bribes from them. If they offered a hundred, I offered a thousand. Thus I taught the goldsmiths to buy [stolen] jewels and pearls. These two were thrown into prison.

The Tatar then had a petition drawn up alleging that I intended to desert the Grand Prince. He said "Yes," and I said "No," but we were not left together. He had to prove it. He then referred to my maid, Anna, and her husband, Hans, as though they knew about it. The maid and her husband were immediately seized on my estate in the zemshchina, and brought before the court. The great princes and the clerks of the oprichnina were scornful of me. One said to another, "Do you want to eat meat?" It was Friday; they meant to butcher me.

When the maid was brought before the court, she spoke properly and truthfully. The senior prince, Vasilii Temkin, asked the maid, "Was your master going to desert the Grand Prince?" The maid held a crucifix before her according to the custom and answered, "By the holy cross, no." Then all the clerks and princes became red with shame, and thought about my money. With the testimony of the maid, I won the case. The Tatar had thought to take over my estate, but with the maid's answer he lost the case. I was thereby acquitted. If the maid had told, however, what she did not know, then torture would have followed and I would have lost.

The Tatar was put into prison. I then rode to my estate, got the maid's husband and brought him before the great lords. He was also asked, and answered "No." Since it was now evening, the great men had the Tatar brought from the prison and said that he was to speak the truth. He now observed that the jailer was present, so he confessed that it was not true. He had accused me because I had had him beaten so severely. In the courtyard the officials were all ready with lanterns, on horse and on foot. If the Tatar had kept to his charge, they would have seized me on my estate during the night and led me away. The next morning I came again before these important persons at the oprichnina court. "There is your servant," the clerk said to me. Now I had the right to take him and have him killed. I answered the clerk Osip Il'in, "I do not want such a servant."

Since my people then asked me to forgive him, I did so and took him on again. Otherwise he would have had to remain in prison and eat pancakes; for the great men could not free him without my permission. When he was at my estate once again and saw that I would not trust him with anything, he denounced me anew and hinted that he wanted to complain to the Grand Prince and say that the boyars acquitted me because I gave them money. I had two sons of boyars[18] constantly with me, Nevezha and his brother Teshata, who told me about this. Thereupon I thought it over quickly, and then had him thrown out the door. Not long afterward he [and another] were caught in a theft. He was beaten to death with a club and then thrown into a river. His companion escaped from prison.

I was again advised that the maid was pilfering a great deal from me. I had a servant, a Livonian named Andrei, who had come to Moscow with a Pole. I put him in the place of the maid. Then, when I noticed that he was acting improperly, I replaced him with the maid again. He tried the following scheme. Stealing my seal, he wrote my steward Ladoe a letter that said, "Ladoe, give Andrei six of the best horses. I have to ride someplace quickly." The letter was not signed by me, but the steward did not read it closely. He therefore gave Andrei the six horses together with a stableboy. [Andrei] took the horses and brought them to the Pole's estate. When the Pole got the horses, he had Andrei chased away. When I learned of this, I asked him through Johann Taube what he had in mind. Seeing that I and Johann Taube were acting together, he gave me so many of his horses that I was satis-

[18] By "sons of boyars," Staden means *deti boiarskie*—petty nobles.

118

fied. The servant died at an empty estate during the plague, and was eaten by dogs.

When the Grand Prince plundered his own country, cities, and villages with his oprichniki, strangling and beating his captives and his enemies to death, this is what happened. Several thousand teamsters were readied with horses and sleighs. On the road, they were in very high spirits.[14] They had to take all the boxes and chests and goods from Great Novgorod to a monastery outside the city. Everything was heaped up here and guarded, so that no one could make off with anything. It was to be equally divided, but that did not happen. When I saw that, I decided not to go campaigning with the Grand Prince.

Then, when the Grand Prince set out for Pskov, a number of merchants from Kholmogory sought my help. They had many packets of sables, and feared that they would be taken. They therefore wanted to make a deal, because the road was occupied and guarded. "Sir, buy our sables. Give us what you want for them," they said. "I have no money with me at present," I replied. "Give us a note," they answered, "we will take payment from you at your house in Moscow." I could have taken those sables without money. I did not do it, because Petr Visloukhii from Pustozersk, who received the yearly sable tribute from the Samoyeds, did business with me and was a good friend of mine. I turned down their offer, and they took another route to England.

I now began to assemble a lot of retainers, especially

[14] The rest of this sentence is so unclear that any translation would be a guess. Epstein admits as much, and Polosin omits it without comment. The sentence reads, *Die waren auf dem zuge übermütigk mit erpessack oder loossen, heist gamagun.*

those menials who were naked and destitute, and I dressed them. The fellows liked this. I then undertook my own expedition. These servants were true to me. When they took a captive from a monastery, house, or church, they politely asked where the money was; and [when they took one from some] other place, they asked where there were good horses. If the prisoner did not want to respond nicely, they held him and tortured him until he told. They therefore got money and goods for me.

Now we came to a place with a church. My servants went inside and plundered it, taking icons and similar foolish things. This was not far from the estate of a prince in the zemshchina where three hundred armed men were assembled. I alone remained mounted. [I then saw] six horsemen chased by the three hundred zemskie people. I did not know whether they were zemskie people or oprichniki. I called my servants from the church to their horses. Only then did I understand the situation correctly: the six were from the oprichnina, and they were pursued by the three hundred zemskie people. They called to me for help and I advanced. When the zemskie people saw so many men coming out of the church, they turned back toward the estate. I shot one dead immediately, forced my way through them, and quickly went through the gates. Here they threw stones from the upper floors. I took one of my servants, Teshata, and we ran up the stairs. I had an axe in my hand. I was then met by a princess who wanted to throw herself at my feet. Seeing my angry face, she turned to go back into the room. I struck her in the back with the axe and she fell through the doorway. Then I sprang over her and greeted her ladies.

When I hurried from the women's room to the court, the six oprichniki fell at my feet saying: "Thank you, sir, for saving our lives just now. We will inform our master about it, and he will tell the Grand Prince how nobly you have borne yourself against the zemskie people. We saw your caution and bravery with our own eyes." "Take what you can, and hurry," I said to my servants.

I then rode the entire night and came to an unfortified settlement. I did not harm anyone here, I just rested. After two days of lying quietly, I learned that five hundred harquebusiers of the oprichnina had been killed by the zemskie people at that place. I subsequently arrived in the court of my estate called Nova. I sent the goods to Moscow.

I went campaigning with the Grand Prince, three of us with one horse, and returned with 49 [horses], 22 with wagons full of goods. The Grand Prince then came to the city of Staritsa, where he mustered his forces in order to see how they had borne up and how many remained with him. The Grand Prince then said to me, "You shall be called Andrei Volodimirovich." The word "vich" means princely and noble.[15] Previously I had been compensated with the princes and boyars. With these words the Grand Prince gave me to understand that I was now a noble. In this country a foreigner has the best place, if he knows how to live according to the country's customs for a while.

The Grand Prince went to Aleksandrova Sloboda, and had churches built. I did not go with him, but went to Moscow. There all the princes and boyars who sat in

---

[15] Of course, "vich" is not "princely and noble" as Staden asserts; "Volodimirovich" is merely a patronymic.

the court of the oprichnina were depressed. They were fearful because of their treason.

After the Grand Prince had built these churches, the plague still ruled the country. I arrived at the oprichnina court. Everything was quiet. The chief persons looked at me peevishly and asked, "What do you want here? Is everything dying at your place too?" "No, thank God," I said. They again asked what I wanted there. I then realized that all the servants of these gentlemen had been released during the famine, and I had taken many of them on. I thought of the Grand Prince's words, "You shall be named Andrei Volodimirovich," and therefore acted according to my rank.

I started a business with Hartmann Krugmann, a citizen of Aschersleben in the bishopric of Halberstadt. If he had not dealt with me dishonestly and had returned to Moscow, I would have been able to get a position in the sable treasury. I could have used such a position to my advantage, so that when I returned to the Christian world I would have led the life of a nobleman. "Now, since it is impossible," I said to myself, "you must return. You cannot go any higher."

Because of money, I had to study Russian law. My maid Anna's husband then came to me. I had entrusted all my possessions to them, and he had certainly profited from this. He thought to defend what he had stolen from me. He had a petition submitted that accused me of compelling him with force to give me a promissory note. This was customary, since no one is permitted to hold a servant [against his will], and no one does. A servant must give his master a note or he is not taken on. One bondage is complete. The usual [promissory note] reads thus: "I, N., acknowledge that I have received money from this person." The interest is then set at one to five [20 per cent]. If one has a servant or a maid who has not given a note, the servant is quite free to steal from his master and run off before his eyes as well. If a servant or maid has given a promissory note, no one [else] can take him on, and if [the master] lays hands on him, he is treated lightly by the law. If he should run away and try to enroll as a harquebusier in the oprichnina, I would then come and would not permit it. It was not commanded that the servants of oprichnina princes and boyars should enlist as harquebusiers.

The servant then took a caftan as a pledge from a harquebusier of the [oprichnina] court who did not have money to pay for what he had drunk. This harquebusier fled. Now my servant was arrested and brought bound before the law. The servant was asked who his master was. He answered, "My master is Andrei Volodimirovich." I was immediately called before the law. The captain of the harquebusiers said, "A harquebusier has been killed in this house. The Grand Prince does not want to lose him. He had gold and money with him, sixty rubles. Have him give me back the money." The caftan was presented and the decision came quickly: I had to pay. The other harquebusiers were happy, and wanted to take me before the law at once and beat me on the legs with clubs. The gentlemen [of the court] said, "Do not beat him. Let him alone until he gets the money." When I laid the money on the table, the captain of the harquebusiers said, "I did not realize that I asked for so little. I should have demanded a thousand." My servant was then freed and given over to me. The gentlemen said, "Take your servant and do what you want with him."

When I arrived at my estate, I had him hung by his hands in a room. "Master, let me go," he begged. "I will get your money for you again." "Then do it!" I an-

swered. He took a shirt and placed one of my golden
bowls in it and went to a man who dealt in malt. It was
said that my maid had deposited with this man some of
the money stolen from me. When he came into the house,
the housewife wanted to keep the shirt for him. He
watched closely where she put the shirt. I then had my
servant arrested and brought him before the law. I requested that the gentlemen assign witnesses to me, for I
knew where the money that the servant had stolen had
been put. The gentlemen assigned them. Then, when we
came to the house where the shirt with the golden bowl
was, the servant was stripped naked and led into every
corner. The housewife, seeing what was happening,
screamed and cried. When the servant found the shirt in
the presence of the witnesses, it was immediately sealed.
I soon won the case. The housewife was brought before
the court.

I was ashamed to accuse this woman, because she had
been my close neighbor in the zemshchina. Her former
husband had been an artist. I said, "Gentlemen, at present it is too late to bring the charge." The gentlemen ordered the woman to be kept in custody in order that she
be present when I accused her. The judge, Dmitrii Pi-
vov, was on my side, and he was pleased that I got my
money back. He knew well that the captain of the harquebusiers had accused me falsely and had unjustly taken
the money from me. Now I was in a position to get the
money back, but I did not—for the reason [mentioned
above].

Chilibei, a merchant of the Turkish Sultan, had to
leave Moscow quickly, and the Grand Prince commanded all those who owed him money to pay their debts.
Aleksei Basmanov then asked me to lend him fifty ru-

bles. When I gave him the money, he came with a golden chain, wanting to give it to me as a pledge, but I did not want it. Learning of this, his son Fedor came to me. He was the one with whom the Grand Prince indulged in lewdness, and that year he was the senior field commander when the oprichnina fought the Crimean Khan. "In what district is your estate?" he asked affably. "In Staritsa, sir," I answered. "That district is presently assigned to me," he said. "Do not take any provisions with you. You shall eat at my table and your servants with mine." I thanked him but refused. "Do you not want to come?" he asked. "I am powerful and can defend you well, as you yourself know." I then refused him cheerfully and went away in good spirits. Some of our people ridiculed me.

When this gentleman [Fedor] returned home, the Grand Prince gave him a princess. I was also invited to the wedding. The Grand Prince was very gay at this wedding. This gentleman [Fedor] said to me, "What do you desire? Tell me and it will be yours at once, because the Grand Prince is cheerful. I will tell him what a true heart you have in your bosom." I then declined with thanks and said, "At present, thank God, I need nothing. I only ask that you remain gracious to me." He looked around and ordered that the money I loaned be repaid. It was returned in a sealed sack.

A boyar named Fedor Sanin saw this. He had been in many foreign countries. He quite affably asked me to ride with him. When I came to the house, all the usual deference was shown me. He went with me into a room, where I saw much money and goods. "Are you married?" he asked. "No," I answered. "Let us go see my daughter," he said. "If you marry her, I will give you what you wish, as much money and property as you desire." I refused him with thanks and answered that I had enough money and property and therefore did not want to get married.

During the plague, when all the roads and highways were guarded, one of the peasants in my village died, and so did his wife, children, and entire household, except for a small girl. My bailiffs had the property recorded in the presence of other sworn authorities and provided it with a guard. A peasant named Nikita Lykoshin then came and declared that he had been the lover of the [deceased] woman. Those who were guarding the property said that at present nothing would be resolved, either here or elsewhere. "If you want something, then go to Moscow!" He well knew that one could neither go to Moscow nor come from there [because of the plague]. He therefore resorted to his own tricks and took everything by force. Although the road was guarded, I learned of this. I sent a petition secretly and with care, [by a route] where there was no guard, and had him summoned before the law for the first time. I then summoned him a second and a third time. He still did not appear. The guards were then removed from all cities and roads, and I sent and had him arrested. He was drunk when this happened. He was then bound, and I ordered that he be stoutly beaten in the marketplace in the city of Staritsa, so that he would give me bail; but no one wanted to put up his bail, both because he was rich and because they did not want to offend me. In addition, he had my property.

I then made plans to get his property as well as my property. He was so stubborn that he would give up neither his nor mine. He was then put in chains welded with lead, and was led to Moscow. In Moscow he was entrusted to the nedel'shchiki. With them he had to be servant, maid, and boy, and was beaten every day in the marketplace, according to custom. I came from Aleksandrova Sloboda to Moscow and observed this affair. This Nikita Lykoshin became happy and sad,[16] and he had a petition drawn up in which he requested that he be given over to me as my serf until he paid. The gentlemen [of the court] then asked me, "Do you want to take this man and have him chastised? If so, we will give him to you. When you have been paid, you must present him to us again." I now got guarantees and took him away. I sent him to my estate Nova. Here he was so treated by my household that he could no longer stand up to the punishment. He was heard to say that he wanted to kill himself at night, because he could no longer bear the beatings and scorn. I considered this quickly and then ordered an iron collar made for him with a chain six feet long. The chain could be fastened to the collar so that he could lie down at night and sit or stand during the day. I also ordered that hand irons be made for him in order to bind both his hands together. He was therefore prevented from killing himself. He could then be set free in the morning and be led to the square and punished. The irons were welded with lead. I also ordered that he not be beaten so severely, because he might die. After standing in the village square for a quarter of an hour, subjected to all kinds of scorn and blows, he was returned to his place. This occurred daily on my estate. Still he would not submit. He called out my name every day in a loud voice when he was beaten, "Gospodar Andrei

---

[16] *Froh und traurigk.* Perhaps he was happy in the hope of escaping the nedel'shchiki and sad about his lot.

Volodimirovich, pozhalui menia!"—that is, Lord Andrei Volodimirovich, pardon me! He intended to suffer
this way until I let him go.

The village where the peasant lived was not far from
my estate. His son was a good fellow, carousing and
swearing around the clock and he always had a secret
love affair. He went to his father and admonished him
to remain steadfast. He did that without once offering to
give anything. "Master, send and have everything that
belongs to me brought from the village," [the father]
said. "That is not worth the bother to me," I answered.
"Have your son sell everything and pay me. Do you
think I do not have enough clubs to smash your legs?"
Although they beat him so that he could no longer stand
and had to lie down, still he called my name every day.

When I returned from Moscow, there was a commoner with me named Ulrich Krugmann, who presently
lives under the Prince of Anhalt in Könnern. He wanted
very much to return home, but did not know how to do
it. When he heard of this [affair], he begged me, "Dear
Heinrich von Staden, pardon him on my account. Take
something from the man and give it to me for provisions,
and let the man go." I did this and also let [Krugmann]
choose two of the best horses in my stable, and a servant.
Although the peasant should have given me 260 rubles,
he gave me only ten then. I gave them and the horses to
[Krugmann] and sent him close to Livonia where he
might be able to leave the country. In this I was risking
my life; for if they were caught, I would have either
been hanged or thrown into the river. No one is allowed
out of the country without a pass or the permission of the
Grand Prince. How he repaid me is too long to explain
here.

When the Crimean Khan arrived outside Moscow, no one could leave the city. As the fire got the upper hand, I wanted to run into a cellar. In front of the cellar was a German girl from Livonia who said to me, "The cellar is full. You cannot come in." In the cellar, there were mainly Germans who served the Grand Prince, together with their wives and children. I then saw my servant Herman from Lübeck up in the vault of the cellar. I beat my way through the Russians and came to the vault, which had an iron door. I chased half [of the people] out of the vault and put my entire household inside. Meanwhile the fire from the oprichnina court spread to the Kremlin and to the entire city.

I had acquired three miners for the Grand Prince, at his wish and command but at my own expense. I then saw one, named Andreas Wolff, trying to put out the fire as it burned everywhere around him. I sprang from the vault and dragged him in with me and immediately shut the iron door. When the fire was past, I looked to see how it was in the cellar below. Everyone who was there was dead and charred from the flames. The cellar was filled knee deep with water.

In the next year [1572], when the soldiers of the Grand Prince were all together on the Oka River, each one, according to the extent of his estates, had to assist in the construction of the barricade of wagons, and each had to help dig entrenchments on the banks of the Oka by the cord.[17] I did not want to do it. Then, when the Khan got to the Oka River, Prince Dmitrii Khvorostinin —who was commander of the advance regiment—sent

---

[17] That is, the entrenchments were four feet wide, four feet deep, and eight feet long.

me off with three hundred princes and boyars. I was to look for the point where the Khan would cross the river. I went several miles upstream and there I saw several thousand of the Crimean Khan's horsemen on my side of the river. I advanced with the three hundred horses and immediately sent a dispatch to Prince Dmitrii asking him to come and help. "If things are not going well, it would be better for you to return to us," Prince Dmitrii answered. This was impossible, for the Khan's troops had encircled us with several thousand men, and had forced us to the Oka. My horse was shot dead from under me. I sprang over the entrenchment into the river, for the bank here was steep. All three hundred were slaughtered. The Khan proceeded with great strength along the bank, and I alone remained alive.

As I sat on the bank, two fishermen came up and said, "Perhaps that is a Tatar. Let's kill him." "I am no Tatar," I answered. "I serve the Grand Prince and have my estates in the district of Staritsa." Two beautiful horses appeared on the other side of the river. They had run away from the Tatars. I asked them if they would take me across the river so that I might get a horse again. When I got across to the horses, no one could catch them.

When this game[18] was over, all the estates were given back to the zemskie people, because they had resisted the Khan of the Crimea. The Grand Prince could no longer do without them. Those in the oprichnina were to be given other estates in exchange. I lost my pomestia and votchiny because of this, and I was no longer registered in the muster book of the princes and boyars. The reason for this is that all Germans were registered to-

[18] *Dis spil*—that is, the campaign on the Oka in 1572.

gether in one muster book. The Germans thought I was registered with the princes and boyars in the oprichnina. The princes and boyars thought I was registered with the other Germans. I was therefore forgotten in the mustering.

After a while, giving up everything, I went and built a mill at Rybnaya Sloboda, and carefully considered how I might leave the country.

I was well acquainted with David Kondin, who collected tribute in Lapland. When I went to Lapland, I declared that I was waiting for a merchant who owed me a sum of money. Here I encountered Dutchmen. I behaved as though I were a great merchant, and became a broker between Dutchmen, Englishmen, Norwegians from Bergen, and Russians.

The Russians here wanted to argue with me, saying that their religion was better than the Germans'. I answered that ours was better than theirs. For this the Russians wanted to throw me into the Kola River. Jacob Heine from Schiedam, Johann von Rohma and Johann Jacob from Antwerp, and Severin and Michael Falck from Norway would not stand for this. When I saw this, I pretended I was feebleminded. Then no one paid any more attention to me.

When we came to Ameland, we ran into a strong wind and a storm from the northeast. It threw us onto Ameland and forced us up a hostile river. Three galleys manned by Walloons then appeared. "Dear brothers," we cried, "save us from our troubles. We would gladly go to Flanders." "Yes," they said, thinking we were their own people. Only when we were again at sea did they realize that we wanted to go to Holland.

When I arrived in Holland, I took a Russian and went

to Heinrich Kramer and Caspar Schelhammer in Leipzig. They both thought they would like to begin trading with the Russians on the coast I described. They sent several thousand jewels set in gold with the Russian to be sold to the Treasury of the Grand Prince.

I set off for Holland with five hundred zentner of cannon balls.[19] As I was again leaving Holland, I was arrested near 's Hertogenbosch. The count wanted to torture and hang me. After three days I was released.

When I again arrived in Germany, I undertook my trip to the King of Sweden. I asked the King for a pass in order to fetch what the Grand Prince owed me on the seacoast [I] described. The King ordered that I be given three passes. When the passes were signed and sealed, the chancellor said, "Give us a guarantee." Although the chancellor had been captured by the Russians at Narva and had lost both feet from frostbite, he still wanted to spare the enemy. If I had wanted to give a thousand talers, no guarantee would have been necessary. The chancellor was called Wenzeslaus. He gave the three passes to a man named Gert Friese who was born under the count of Emden in East Frisia. When I arrived in Emden and demanded the passes, he informed Duke Charles, the brother of the King of Sweden. The three passes were then denied me.

Duke Charles thought I would serve him. He therefore sent me into Holland, where I was to see if there were any Russian merchants. He wanted to capture them at sea. When I returned to East Frisia, Duke Charles had gone off to visit his brother-in-law Duke Georg Hans, the Count of the Palatinate.

[19] In the manuscript, this sentence and the preceding paragraph stand before the paragraph above them, out of chronological order.

When I arrived in Lützelstein and reported to Duke Charles concerning the Russian trade, the Count of the Palatinate took me aside and asked me about the Grand Prince and about conditions in his country. He kept me for a few months, and [then] sent me to the King of Poland. I carried out my orders with great diligence and according to my instructions. He later sent me to the German Master and then to your Imperial Roman Majesty. In Moscow I wanted to come to you very much and I often asked the Grand Prince for permission. Thank the Almighty God who considered me worthy to experience this.

Later I could certainly write down how Livonia was ruled by the deceased Master [of the Livonian Order], how it was lost through such a rule, and how it could be reconquered and kept from its hereditary foe, the Grand Prince. I am prepared to do this obediently, if that is your Imperial Roman Majesty's wish and desire.

Index